Nailed It!!!

(A metaphysical translation of Bible parables)

Mychael T Renn

Ecclesiastes 12:12, Of making many books there is no end, and much study is wearisome to the flesh

Disclaimer

These interpretations were not meant to negate or replace traditional biblical understandings but to offer a supplementary spiritual or metaphysical lens through which one might explore the inner, symbolic meanings of the scriptures.

Contents

Preface

In this journey of spiritual discovery, "Nailed It" invites you into a world where the ancient and the modern converge, where biblical stories are reimagined through a metaphysical lens, and where personal narratives intertwine with timeless wisdom. This book is born from a pivotal moment of discovery and a profound journey of transformation, both personal and familial.

In 2018, during a Thanksgiving gathering, a chance encounter with Charles Fillmore's "Metaphysical Bible Dictionary" opened a doorway to a new realm of understanding. This book sat initially as a dormant seed of curiosity, overshadowed by life's unfolding dramas, including a divorce and a subsequent move. However, like the most resilient of seeds, it eventually found fertile ground in a period of personal transition and introspection. Rediscovered, it became a beacon, guiding me and my daughters through the metaphysical landscapes of biblical narratives.

The journey that unfolds in these pages is unique. It transcends the traditional interpretation of biblical tales, infusing them with a metaphysical understanding that speaks to the heart of modern existential quests. Each chapter illustrates how ancient wisdom can illuminate our understanding of human nature and inspire spiritual growth. The dialogues with my daughters breathe life into these texts, showing how these stories resonate within our everyday lives.

This book is not merely an academic exercise; it's a chronicle of a family's journey through the realms of ancient wisdom and modern insights. It is an invitation to readers to explore, question, and find personal meaning in these timeless narratives. Join us in this exploration of love, faith, understanding, and growth as we continue to learn, evolve, and unfold within the infinite spiral of spiritual discovery. And now about me.....In the web of life, every strand represents a journey, a lesson, or a transformation waiting to unfold. My name is Mychael T. Renn, and the fabric of my life has been woven with colors both dark and vibrant, each hue a testament to a journey of recovery, discovery, and fatherhood. This book is not merely a collection of narratives; it is a portal into the soulful odyssey of a man who once danced with shadows but found his way to the light through the unyielding power of love, family, and self-discovery.

Divorced and navigating the turbulent waters of single fatherhood, I found myself in the depths of addiction, my life defined by the next job, the next high, the relentless cycle of a Boilermaker entrenched in the union welder's life. Yet, it was in the fragility of this existence that I discovered an immutable truth: we are not defined by our lowest points but by our courage to rise above them.

The narratives woven into the fabric of this book trace the spiritual and emotional journey that my daughters and I embarked upon, a journey punctuated by moments of profound sadness, indomitable hope, and unbreakable love. From the industrial landscapes of St. Louis, where loss and despair threatened to consume us, to the sun-drenched shores of Miami, where salvation in the form of a pen and paper awaited, our story is one of transformation.

As a family, we grew not just in proximity but in the depths of our souls. The move to St. Louis, though fraught with challenges, including the loss of my job, became the catalyst for a profound personal and collective awakening. It was in the crucible of these trials that I shed the skin of my former self—a drug-addicted welder—emerging as a beacon of hope, not only for my daughters but for anyone who has ever lost their way in the darkness.

Today, I stand before you, a changed man. The vices that once held me in their grip are no longer chapters in my story. I have embraced a life of integrity, my body a temple, my mind a sanctuary of peace and philosophical inquiry. The decision to move to Miami and write this book was not merely a change in geography; it was an affirmation of my commitment to a new way of living, to be a father not just in name but in action, and to share the wisdom gleaned from a life reborn.

This book is an invitation to journey with us, to witness the metamorphosis of a man and his family as they navigate the tumultuous yet rewarding path to self-realization and love. It is a testament to the resilience of the human spirit, a reminder that no matter how far we may fall, redemption is always within reach if only we have the courage to grasp it.

In sharing our story, I hope to light a beacon for those still wandering in the night, to offer a hand to those seeking to climb from the depths. Our journey is a testament to the power of transformation, the beauty of second chances, and the enduring strength of familial bonds.

Welcome to our story, a narrative of loss, love, and the unyielding belief that, in the end, we can all find our way home.

Introduction

Welcome to "Nailed It," a narrative where biblical tales are not only studied but lived, where their metaphysical interpretations become the lens through which we view the world, and where a family's journey mirrors the timeless wisdom these stories impart.

My personal journey with these narratives began with serendipitous discovery, leading me through a transformative process that intertwined my life with the metaphysical insights of Charles Fillmore. This book is an embodiment of that journey, shared with my daughters as we navigate the complexities of modern life through the wisdom of ancient texts.

Each chapter in this book is a reflection of our journey, beginning with the traditional narrative and transitioning into its metaphysical interpretation. These stories are then woven into the fabric of our daily lives, creating a dialogue between generations and exploring the spiritual insights and practical wisdom they offer.

In "Nailed It," the metaphysical approach we adopt goes beyond mere intellectual analysis. It is about delving into the archetypes and underlying meanings of biblical stories, transcending time and culture. We explore key narratives from both the Old and New Testaments, revealing their deeper symbolic and spiritual messages, and intertwine these with our personal experiences and insights.

This book is significant because it bridges the gap between ancient wisdom and contemporary experience. It demonstrates the enduring relevance of the Bible's teachings and how they continue to shape our understanding of life, love, faith, and family. Through our shared explorations, we discover how these stories can inform our modern lives, offering guidance and insight for our spiritual and personal growth.

Join us on this journey of exploration as we weave together the metaphysical, the personal, and the familial. Let us explore, learn, and evolve within the infinite spiral of spiritual unfolding, finding new ways to understand and engage with these timeless tales.

Part One
The Old Testament

Chapter One
The Creation Story

Introduction

The Creation story, as found in the Book of Genesis, has intrigued theologians, scholars, and laypeople alike for centuries. It serves as the opening narrative of the Bible and sets the stage for all that follows. In this chapter, we will delve into the metaphysical interpretation of this captivating story to better understand its spiritual and practical applications for our lives.

Traditional Narrative

The biblical account begins with a formless void and darkness covering the deep. Over the course of seven days, God brings the world into existence, culminating in the creation of humankind—Adam and Eve—in His image. Each day of Creation introduces a new element, from the separation of light and darkness to the formation of the Earth's landscapes and creatures.

Biblical Context

Scholars suggest that the Creation story, particularly as described in Genesis, is likely an amalgamation of various Near Eastern myths and traditions. While the story's primary purpose was to define the relationship between God and His Creation, it also served to delineate moral and cultural norms for ancient societies.

Interfaith and Cultural Perspectives

The concept of creation is not unique to Judeo-Christian traditions. Hinduism, for instance, has the concept of 'Brahma' as the creator, while Native American myths often involve a Great Spirit or Earth Mother. The metaphysical themes, although expressed differently, often resonate across these cultural narratives.

Metaphysical Interpretation

Using Charles Fillmore's Metaphysical Bible Dictionary, the seven days of Creation can be viewed as seven stages of spiritual awakening or consciousness development. "Light," for example, signifies divine intelligence or wisdom, while "darkness" can symbolize ignorance or unenlightenment. Adam and Eve embody the masculine and feminine aspects of divine consciousness, representing the balanced spiritual forces necessary for complete understanding.

Quotes and References

Charles Fillmore once said, "The true history of man is the history of his unfoldment in Divine Mind." This statement illuminates the metaphysical interpretation of the Creation story as an account of human potential, divinity, and spiritual journeying.

Real-world Examples

Consider an individual embarking on a spiritual journey—each "day" or phase of their journey could parallel the seven days of Creation. A newfound awareness (light) emerges from a state of ignorance or confusion (darkness), followed by periods of growth, introspection, and eventually enlightenment.

Practical Applications

Readers can apply these insights through mindfulness exercises, focusing on their spiritual "creation" or growth each day. For example, dedicating time to meditating on 'light' can help you cultivate wisdom and clarity.

Reader Reflections

1. How does the metaphysical interpretation of the Creation story resonate with your spiritual beliefs or practices?
2. Can you identify "days" or phases in your life that reflect the seven days of Creation?

Glossary of Metaphysical Interpretations for This Chapter

- Seven Days of Creation: Seven phases of spiritual awakening.
- Light: Divine intelligence or wisdom.
- Darkness: Ignorance or unenlightened state.
- Adam: Masculine aspect of divine consciousness.
- Eve: Feminine aspect of divine consciousness.
- Spirit: The animating life force.
- Earth: Physical plane or material world.
- Sky: Realm of higher consciousness.

Additional Exercises

- Guided meditation focuses on the creation of 'light' within you.
- Journaling activity to reflect on the seven stages of your spiritual journey.

The Creation story, through a metaphysical lens, offers a rich insights into the nature of existence, divinity, and human potential. By understanding these deeper layers, we open ourselves to greater spiritual growth and personal transformation.

Chapter One

The Creation - Illumination Beyond the Lake

The vibrant energy of spring embraced the earth as Michael, Ellery, and Tillie ventured on their familiar path to the tranquil lake beyond their property, enveloped by the tender blossoms of nature in its rebirth. The atmosphere, imbued with a serenity that gently nudged introspective thoughts, became an ideal canvas upon which profound dialogues were often painted by the trio.

Michael, ever the philosophical spirit and seasoned by diverse life experiences, initiated their discourse, merging the tangible beauty surrounding them with the metaphysical depths of the Biblical creation story. His knowledge, honed not only by conventional explorations but also underpinned by intense, personal voyages into the realms of consciousness through psychedelics, rendered his interpretations both rich and vibrantly colorful.

"The creation story," Michael began, absorbing the verdant beauty surrounding them, "isn't merely a tale of Earth's origin. Charles Fillmore, through his metaphysical lens, proposed it as a symbolic narrative detailing the evolution of consciousness within us."

Ellery, with her inherently rebellious yet profoundly introspective spirit, paused, "So, the creation isn't external but an internal metamorphosis, sculpting our inner worlds?"

"That's insightful, Ellery," Michael responded, a gentle smile appearing on his face. "Fillmore indeed envisioned the 'six days of creation' as phases of our personal spiritual development. 'God' is not perceived as an entity external to us, but as an infinite, divine principle, residing within, orchestrating this internal evolution."

Tillie, with her artist's heart and soul, intuitively grasped the symbolic nuances, "So, each 'day' is a metaphorical step where different aspects of our understanding and spiritual faculties are developed and refined?"

"Yes, Tills," Michael affirmed, "The first utterance of 'let there be light' can be seen as an awakening, a spark of awareness, dispelling the shadow of ignorance, and initiating our journey towards understanding our own divine nature."

As they meandered closer to the lake, the shimmering water

reflecting the gentle dance of the sun, Michael pondered a fitting philosophical musing to deepen their reflection. "A quote by Alan Watts comes to mind," he shared, "'You are a function of what the whole universe is doing in the same way that a wave is a function of what the whole ocean is doing.' This echoes the intrinsic connection between our internal evolution and the expansive, universal energies at play in the creation story."

The lake, a serene mirror to the skies, listened silently to their conversation, providing a tranquil backdrop to their explorative dialogue. The trio engaged further into the metaphysical layers of the creation story, uncovering how each metaphorical 'day' symbolized transformative phases of human consciousness and spiritual unfolding.

Ellery, deeply reflective, pondered aloud, "So, our external world, and even our actions, mirror this internal, spiritual evolution?"

"Yes, precisely," Michael confirmed, "and our journey is not linear but an ongoing spiral, where we continually revisit and refine aspects of our understanding, continuously shaping our internal world."

Tillie, her thoughts often finding expression through her artistic creations, mused, "This symbolic interpretation allows the story to be timeless, making it an ever unfolding internal journey."

As the trio, bound by familial ties and a shared journey of spiritual and philosophical explorations, continued their dialogues, the metaphysical interpretation of the creation story melded seamlessly into their collective consciousness. The symbolic, internal creation, framed against the tangible beauty of the world around them, enriched their understanding of the spiritual evolution within.

And there, beside the reflective tranquility of the lake, the first chapter of their exploration was gently woven into the fabric of their ongoing journey, to be carried forward into the chapters to come, within this sacred, familial exploration of spiritual discovery, carefully preserved in their collective, unfolding storybook, "Nailed It."

A Prayer

Heavenly Creator,

You who set the universe in motion and breathed life into all beings,

Open my eyes to the divine wisdom encoded within the story of Creation.

Guide me through the seven days of my spiritual awakening,

From the first glimmers of light in my soul to the complexity of human understanding.

Help me embrace the duality within—light and darkness, masculine and feminine, creator and creation.

Grant me the humility to learn from different traditions and perspectives,

And the courage to venture deeper into the mystery of my own existence.

As I journey through the cycles of my spiritual life,

May each cycle bring me closer to enlightenment, peace, and unity with Your divine plan.

Amen.

Journaling Prompts

1. What are some moments in your life where you've felt a separation of "light" (wisdom, understanding) and "darkness" (ignorance, confusion)? How did you navigate through them?

2. In which "day" or phase of spiritual awakening do you currently find yourself based on the metaphysical interpretation of the Creation story?

3. Have you ever felt like both the creator and the creation in your own life? Explain a situation where you experienced this duality.

4. Which cultural or religious narratives other than the Judeo-Christian Creation story resonate with your own understanding of the world's creation or your spiritual awakening?

5. How do you balance the masculine and feminine aspects of your own divine consciousness? Can you identify a moment where this balance was crucial?

Chapter Two
Adam and Eve and the Fall

Introduction

The story of Adam and Eve, along with their expulsion from the Garden of Eden, serves as one of the most captivating and controversial narratives in the Bible. Commonly understood as an origin story for sin and human suffering, this chapter delves into the metaphysical implications of the tale, shedding new light on the lessons it holds for personal growth and spiritual understanding.

Traditional Narrative

In the Book of Genesis, Adam and Eve live in the Garden of Eden, a paradise where they have access to every tree except the Tree of Knowledge of Good and Evil. Seduced by the serpent, Eve eats the forbidden fruit and shares it with Adam. As a result, they become aware of their nakedness, symbolizing their newfound knowledge and shame. God then banishes them from Eden.

Biblical Context

The story is often read as an allegory for humanity's fall from grace and the onset of mortal life, complete with suffering and death. Biblical scholars also point to its origins in earlier myths and its role in explaining moral and social norms in early Judeo-Christian communities.

Interfaith and Cultural Perspectives

Various religious traditions interpret the story differently. In Islamic thought, Adam and Eve are forgiven by God and their "fall" is considered more of a descent into earthly existence than a moral failure. Certain Eastern philosophies share a similar perspective, viewing the story as an allegory for spiritual awakening rather than sinfulness.

Metaphysical Interpretation

Turning to Charles Fillmore's Metaphysical Bible Dictionary, the Garden of Eden represents a state of pristine consciousness, while Adam and Eve symbolize the dual forces of human awareness: intellect (Adam) and emotion (Eve). The "fall" can be interpreted as the disruption of this balanced state, leading to ego-driven existence and separation from divine consciousness.

Quotes and References

Charles Fillmore observed, "The 'fall of man' is his descent from the purely spiritual consciousness into material consciousness." This provides a framework for understanding the metaphysical "fall" as a shift in focus from the spiritual to the material realm.

Real-world Examples

The balancing act between intellect and emotion is a struggle everyone faces. In relationships, careers, or personal choices, we constantly navigate between rational thought and emotional impulse, echoing the metaphysical themes in the story of Adam and Eve.

Practical Applications

Meditation or mindfulness exercises aimed at balancing intellect and emotion can offer practical ways to incorporate this story's lessons into daily life. By seeking harmony between these two aspects, you can approach a more balanced, conscious existence.

Reader Reflections

1. How does the metaphysical understanding of Adam and Eve's "fall" change your perspective on your own life's challenges?
2. Can you think of moments where the struggle between intellect and emotion impacted your choices?

Concluding Thoughts

The story of Adam and Eve offers profound metaphysical lessons about balance, consciousness, and human nature. When interpreted through this lens, it becomes a story not of sin and punishment but of learning, growth, and the ongoing journey toward spiritual wholeness.

Glossary of Metaphysical Interpretations for This Chapter

- Garden of Eden: State of pristine consciousness.
- Adam: Intellectual aspect of human awareness.
- Eve: Emotional aspect of human awareness.
- The Fall: Descent into ego-driven, material consciousness.
- Tree of Knowledge: Symbol of duality and moral complexity.
- Serpent: Catalyst for change and awakening.
- Forbidden Fruit: The act that disrupts spiritual harmony.

Additional Exercises

1. Guided meditation focuses on harmonizing your intellectual and emotional sides.
2. Journaling activity to reflect on moments of imbalance and how they shaped your spiritual journey.

Chapter Two

The Ethereal Fall Amidst Morning Aromas

The gentle embrace of an early fall morning caressed the world outside as Michael navigated through the familiar motions in the kitchen. The sizzle of bacon - one pan dedicated to Tillie's preferred squishy kind and the other ensuring Ellery's leanings towards a crispier variant were honored - harmonized with the rich aroma of freshly brewed coffee.

As the girls nestled comfortably at the kitchen island, an intimate atmosphere naturally entwined with the scent of cooking enveloped them, providing a warm cocoon where their frequent philosophical and spiritual explorations unfolded.

Michael, ever the seeker of deeper meanings and with an esoteric understanding refined by diverse life experiences, softly introduced the topic for the morning's discourse, "Today, let's delve into the story of Adam and Eve, exploring not the surface tale, but peeling back the layers to reveal the metaphysical insights beneath."

Tillie, with eyes that subtly mirrored the layers of wisdom and curiosity within her, considered the statement. "I've always wondered about the deeper meaning of the 'fall' – it can't just be a simplistic moral about disobedience, can it?"

"Certainly not, Tills," Michael, flipping a biscuit in the pan, responded. "Using Charles Fillmore's metaphysical interpretations, Adam and Eve can be perceived as symbols representing the faculties of our conscious and subconscious minds, respectively."

Ellery, mature beyond her years, partially thanks to the

rebellious path she had carved, mulled over this, "So the Garden of Eden, and the subsequent 'fall,' would then symbolize processes or stages within our consciousness rather than an external event?"

Precisely, Ellery," Michael affirmed, placing meticulously cooked bacon strips onto the biscuits. "The Garden symbolizes a state of consciousness where the soul is in harmonious union with the divine spirit. The 'fall' isn't a punishment for disobedience but represents a shift from spiritual consciousness to self-consciousness or egocentricity."

He paused, ensuring the eggs were softly yet thoroughly cooked, then continued, "Consider this quote from Ralph Waldo Emerson: 'The creation of a thousand forests is in one acorn.' In a way, the fall signifies the dispersion of that singular spiritual consciousness into manifold experiences and learnings, opening up a plethora of pathways to navigate, explore, and eventually, to grow from."

Tillie, gently playing with a strand of her hair while absorbing the philosophical layers, ventured, "So, the eating of the fruit symbolizes our indulgence in the physical and material, thereby forgetting our divine origin and true nature?"

Michael nodded approvingly, "Yes, and the resulting feelings of shame, fear, and guilt that Adam and Eve experienced reflect our own internal turmoil when we lose touch with our intrinsic divine nature, venturing too deeply into materialistic pursuits."

As Michael plated the breakfast, each detail catered to the specific likes of his daughters, Ellery contemplated further, "This interpretation, then, renders the story timeless and universally relevant. Every individual, at some point, experiences this shift or 'fall' from unadulterated spiritual consciousness to self-consciousness, navigating through the myriad experiences, trials, and tribulations life presents."

Michael, handing the plates to his daughters, agreed, "Indeed, E. And our shared explorations, these dialogues, are part of our collective journey to navigate through, understand, and hopefully, glean wisdom from these metaphorical tales, aligning them with our own spiritual and life journeys."

The trio, amidst the savory bites of their morning feast, continued to weave through the metaphysical interpretations of the story, finding reflections of their own journeys within the timeless parable. As the day outside blossomed fully into being, inside, their insightful dialogues gracefully melded into their collective spiritual exploration, gently scripting the second chapter into their unfolding narrative, "Nailed It."

A Prayer

Dear Creator of All,

You who crafted the tale of Adam and Eve,
A story so rich in allegory and metaphysical meaning,
Guide me through the complexities and dualities of my own
existence.

Help me to balance my intellect and emotions,
To embrace the "serpents" that challenge me,
And to view each "fall" as an opportunity for growth and
awakening.

May I always strive for the Eden within me,
A state of consciousness that transcends ego and material
desire.
Grant me the wisdom to navigate my life's garden,
Learning from each tree, each fruit, each fork in the path.

In Your infinite wisdom and compassion,
Amen.

Chapter Three
Cain and Abel

Introduction

The story of Cain and Abel, the sons of Adam and Eve, serves as a poignant continuation of the human narrative begun in the Garden of Eden. Often interpreted as a cautionary tale about jealousy and fratricide, this chapter explores the metaphysical layers hidden within the story, providing insights into the dynamics of human relationships, self-worth, and spiritual growth.

Traditional Narrative

Cain, the elder son, is a farmer, while Abel is a shepherd. Both bring offerings to God, but only Abel's offering is accepted. Enraged by this, Cain kills Abel. When questioned by God, Cain retorts, "Am I my brother's keeper?" God then marks Cain and banishes him, although offering him some protection from others.

Biblical Context

The story is one of the earliest narratives dealing with human conflict and morality in the Bible. Scholars note that it reflects societal tensions between agricultural and pastoral communities, as well as broader themes like justice, punishment, and divine preference.

Interfaith and Cultural Perspectives

The story of Cain and Abel finds parallels in other religious traditions and myths. For instance, the Hindu epic Mahabharata contains themes of fraternal conflict and jealousy, albeit with different outcomes and lessons.

Metaphysical Interpretation

Using Charles Fillmore's Metaphysical Bible Dictionary, Cain and Abel can be seen as representing two different aspects of human consciousness. Cain symbolizes the ego or intellectual mind, driven by material concerns, while Abel symbolizes the heart or spiritual intuition, which is more aligned with divine will.

Quotes and References

Fillmore observed that Cain represents the "human consciousness that is trained in materiality." This provides a lens to view Cain's actions as arising from a materialistic or ego-driven mindset, contrasting with Abel's more spiritual approach.

Real-world Examples

Consider conflicts that arise in families or friendships due to differing values or perspectives. These conflicts often mirror the Cain and Abel dynamic, where one party (akin to Cain) may feel overlooked or undervalued, leading to emotional turmoil.

Practical Applications

Conscious conflict resolution practices, which involve acknowledging both intellectual and emotional aspects of a situation, can help in resolving Cain and Abel-like conflicts in your life. This balance allows for a more spiritually aligned response to challenges.

Reader Reflections

1. Can you recall a situation where you felt overlooked or unappreciated, like Cain? How did you handle it?
2. Are there aspects of your life where you can cultivate more of Abel's qualities, such as spiritual alignment or compassion?

Concluding Thoughts

The story of Cain and Abel, when viewed metaphysically, sheds light on the internal dynamics that influence human behavior. It is less a story of good versus evil and more a narrative about the complexities of human consciousness and the journey toward spiritual maturity.

Glossary of Metaphysical Interpretations for This Chapter

- Cain: Ego or intellectual mind focused on material concerns.
- Abel: Heart or spiritual intuition aligned with divine will.
- Offering: Symbolic act of devotion or surrender.
- Mark of Cain: Protective but isolating influence of ego-driven actions.

Additional Exercises

1. A guided meditation focusing on harmonizing the Cain and Abel aspects within you.
2. Journaling prompts that encourage you to explore conflicts in your life from both an emotional (Abel-like) and intellectual (Cain-like) perspective

Chapter Three

Tracing Legacies under the Overpass

Under the dull grey of the overpass, with the intermittent whoosh of semis far beneath them and the sporadic honks that punctuated the fall air, Michael, Ellery, and Tillie found themselves engulfed in a bubble of vibrant color and contemplative stillness. The cans of spray paint, forming a sporadic palette on the concrete ground, were their tools for expression, rebellion, and collective memory-making.

Tillie, shaking a can of teal spray paint, found a rhythm in the repetitive clinking inside it. She was about to add another layer to her intricate mandala when Michael, recognizing that contemplative look in her eyes, steered the day's conversation towards another archetypal story of familial ties and conflict - Cain and Abel.

"You know," Michael began, his own can paused mid-motion, "The story of Cain and Abel often revolves around themes of jealousy, conflict, and consequence, but there's a deeper, metaphysical interpretation we might explore."

Ellery, ever the seeker of wisdom through understanding, asked, "Is there an insight, Dad, into why Cain's offering was not accepted by God while Abel's was?"

Michael, etching abstract patterns onto the concrete, pondered, "Charles Fillmore interpreted 'Cain' and 'Abel' as symbolizing two aspects within us. Cain represents our physical or outer self, concerned with material, tangible offerings, while Abel represents our inner, spiritual self, which brings offerings of love and devotion."

Tillie, a gentle frown casting shadows upon her youthful features, interjected, "It's like Abel's offering came from a place of genuine, internal abundance, while Cain's perhaps rooted in obligation or societal expectation, even though both brought forth something."

"Indeed, Tills," Michael affirmed. "Leo Tolstoy once said, 'Everyone thinks of changing the world, but no one thinks of changing himself.' The story, in a way, is a reflection of the internal battle within us between the physical and the spiritual, the tangible and the intangible."

Ellery, absorbing the landscape of spray paint dancing in vibrant patterns on the solid, lifeless structure, found a metaphor within. "So, it's like this bridge and the art we create upon it; the bridge, a necessary, tangible structure, and our art, an expression of our internal, intangible world."

"Yes," Michael agreed, "and just like Cain and Abel, both aspects are integral parts of our being. It's not about negating the material for the spiritual or vice versa, but understanding and cultivating a harmonious relationship between the two."

Tillie's thoughts drifted momentarily towards her job at the local pizza place, where the tangible pressures of a demanding boss and the meticulous counting of pennies often eclipsed the intangible joys of connection and shared stories. It was a constant dance between the Cains and Abels within her.

"The tragedy," Michael continued, "lies not in Cain's offering but in his inability to reconcile with the rejection and his subsequent actions stemming from anger and bitterness. His punishment, to be a restless wanderer, can be seen as a disconnection from his spiritual self, constantly seeking but never truly finding."

The three of them, surrounded by their colorful contributions to the otherwise stoic bridge, found a moment of silent reflection amidst the sounds of distant vehicles and the soft whispers of the wind.

In that collective silence, the metaphysical interpretations of Cain and Abel quietly interwove with their personal, internal landscapes. The complexities of their individual and shared journeys – the material struggles and spiritual explorations – found a gentle pause in the underbelly of that overpass, immortalized for a moment in the vibrant splatters of paint on cold, unyielding concrete.

And so, the third chapter gently folded into their ongoing narrative, embedding itself into the colorful, chaotic mural of their shared explorations and silent understandings in their storybook, "Nailed It."

A Prayer:

Dear Heavenly Creator,

We come before you today seeking the wisdom to balance the dual aspects of our nature—the intellect and the spirit, the Cain and the Abel within us. Grant us the courage to confront our egos and the strength to nurture our spiritual selves.

Guide us in the sacrifices we make so they may be offerings of genuine intent rather than quests for external validation. Let us not silence the callings of our hearts in the noise of worldly pursuits.

May we carry the marks of our experiences not as burdens but as lessons—each a stepping stone on our path to spiritual maturity and redemption.

In Your name, we pray,

Amen.

Journaling Prompts:

1. Reflect on a time when you felt your 'Cain' and 'Abel' were in conflict within you. What were the circumstances, and how did you manage this internal struggle?

2. Have you ever made a 'sacrifice' or offering in your life (time, effort, material goods) with the primary motive of seeking validation rather than out of genuine intent? How did that make you feel?

3. When have you experienced a moment of 'divine judgment,' or consequential outcomes, from acting out of ego-driven motives or material concerns? What lessons did you learn?

4. Are there instances where you've silenced your inner 'Abel,' the compassionate and spiritually intuitive aspect of yourself? What prompted this, and how has it affected you?

5. Considering the 'mark of Cain' as a symbol of both your consequences and potential for growth, what 'marks' do you carry? How have they shaped your journey toward spiritual maturity?

Chapter Four
Noah and the Flood

Introduction

The narrative of Noah and the Flood is one of the most iconic stories in the Bible. It is often seen as a tale of judgment and divine retribution, but through a metaphysical lens, it can also offer insights into the cycles of life, purification, and the human journey toward enlightenment.

Traditional Narrative

In this tale, God, disheartened by humanity's wickedness, decides to wipe out life on Earth using a great flood. However, God finds one righteous man—Noah—and instructs him to build an ark to preserve life. After 40 days and nights of rain, the floodwaters recede, and life begins anew.

Biblical Context

The Flood narrative serves multiple functions, including as an etiological myth explaining natural phenomena and as a moral lesson on the consequences of societal decay and disobedience to divine order.

Interfaith and Cultural Perspectives

Similar flood myths exist in various cultures and religions around the world, such as the Sumerian Epic of Gilgamesh. These stories often have themes of divine wrath, survival, and renewal.

Metaphysical Interpretation

Using Charles Fillmore's Metaphysical Bible Dictionary as a guide, the flood can be seen as a cleansing of human consciousness, purging negative thoughts and actions and making way for higher forms of understanding. Noah represents the aspect of human consciousness that is attuned to divine wisdom.

Quotes and References

Fillmore mentions that the flood symbolizes "a great mental housecleaning." This perspective allows us to see life's trials not merely as obstacles but as opportunities for spiritual cleansing and growth.

Real-world Examples

Think of times in your life when you felt overwhelmed by "floods"—be they emotional, physical, or societal. These experiences, difficult as they were, may have also served as catalysts for significant personal change and growth.

Practical Applications

Techniques such as mindful reflection or journaling can help you identify the aspects of your life that may need 'cleansing.' These can be attitudes, relationships, or habits that you've outgrown or that no longer serve you.

Reader Reflections

1. Can you think of a 'flood' moment in your own life? How did it transform you?
2. What practices or perspectives help you in times of upheaval or change?

Concluding Thoughts

The story of Noah and the Flood serves as a potent metaphor for the transformative power of life's challenges. Through the lens of metaphysical interpretation, we can appreciate it not just as a tale of survival against the odds but as a narrative of spiritual growth and renewal.

Glossary of Metaphysical Interpretations for This Chapter

- Flood: Cleansing of human consciousness
- Noah: Aspect of human consciousness aligned with divine wisdom
- Ark: Means of salvation or transformation, carrying the seeds for new beginnings.

Additional Exercises

1. A guided meditation focusing on the concept of 'cleansing,' helping you to let go of elements that no longer serve you.
2. Writing prompts to explore what 'arks' exist in your life that can help you navigate through personal 'floods.'

Chapter Four

Ephemeral Echoes over Dolan Lake

With gentle waves lapping against the shoreline and a boundless azure stretched above, Dolan Lake was a canvas painted with strokes of tranquility and vivid memories. Michael, Ellery, and Tillie settled into a serene spot by the water, their fishing lines dancing lightly atop the surface, allowing the environment to envelop them in a peaceful embrace.

As the tranquility of the lake intermingled with the muffled sounds of distant campers and the subtle hum of nature, Michael found himself drifting into tales of his childhood. Tales where his grandmother's laughter echoed through the trees and the smell of breakfast wafted through the crisp morning air from her cherished camper.

Today, however, the past and the present have converged to become a backdrop for exploring another ancient tale. Michael, his eyes reflecting the gentle sparkle of the water, began to weave the narrative of Noah and the flood through the metaphysical lens offered by Charles Fillmore.

"Do you girls remember the story of Noah?" Michael inquired, his voice as smooth and gentle as the lake before them.

Ellery, her fingers thoughtfully twirling a loose strand of her hair, nodded, "It's often seen as a tale of destruction and salvation, isn't it? But Dad, what are we to learn from it, metaphysically speaking?"

Michael, acknowledging her question, cast his gaze across the lake, where every soft ripple seemed to whisper tales from bygone times. "Noah's Ark, from a metaphysical perspective, is more than merely a vessel of salvation from a divine flood. Fillmore offers a view where the ark symbolizes our own awareness, carrying the essence of our being through floods of external thoughts and societal doctrines."

Tillie, always the one to find metaphors in the tangible, remarked, "So, the flood, then, could be seen as overwhelming influences and forces in our lives, threatening to engulf our authentic selves?"

"Yes, Tillie," Michael confirmed with a gentle smile. "And

amid such tempests of external pressures, our ark becomes that inner sanctuary, safeguarding our true selves and spiritual insights."

He paused, then offered a quote from Ralph Waldo Emerson, "'To be yourself in a world that is constantly trying to make you something else is the greatest accomplishment.' The ark can be seen as that fortress of our authenticity, navigating through the incessant downpours of societal, and even internal, expectations."

As the trio quietly contemplated, their fishing lines idly floating in the still water, they felt the profoundness of the metaphor seep into their being. The lake, with its calming presence, seemed to echo the sentiments of the story, inviting them to find tranquility amidst the undulating waves of life's complexities.

Ellery, with her ever-present introspective gaze, observed, "The animals, taken two by two...perhaps they represent aspects of our own nature, our varied thoughts and emotions, being preserved and acknowledged rather than discarded or drowned."

The poignant observation hung in the air, merging with the gentle breezes and distant sounds of life around the lake. In this space, where memories and the present moment intertwined, they found a delicate understanding of the self, understanding that within each of them sailed an ark through floods of myriad experiences and evolving perceptions.

Tillie, gently reeling in her line, pondered on how her own 'ark' sailed through currents of artistic expression and internal explorations, safeguarding her intrinsic self amidst the floods of external validation and critique.

Their lines, although mostly neglected in favor of the rich dialogue, served as gentle reminders of the ebb and flow of life's journeys. And as the sunlight gracefully danced upon the waters of Dolan Lake, the fourth chapter of their spiritual and familial voyage found a quiet harbor within their collective consciousness, ready to be embarked upon once more in tales to come from their storybook, "Nailed It."

A Prayer

Dear Divine Spirit,

Guide me through the floods of life, through times of challenge and overwhelming emotion. Help me to find my inner Noah, the wisdom and resilience that will steer me toward safety and enlightenment. May I embrace these trials as opportunities for cleansing and growth, trusting that the ark within me carries the seeds for new beginnings?

As I navigate the tempestuous waters, let me not forget the promise of renewal, the new dawn that waits beyond the storm. Like the dove that returns with a sign, may I, too, find symbols of hope, evidence that a better, more enlightened version of myself is emerging from these trials.

In this quest for balance and spiritual completion, I ask for your guidance, your strength, and your eternal wisdom.

Amen.

Journaling Prompts

1. Describe a moment in your life that felt like a "flood," overwhelming you with challenges or emotions. What did you learn from this experience?

2. If your current challenges were likened to a flood, what would be your "ark"—the resilience, resources, or wisdom—that helps you navigate through it?

3. In the context of personal growth, what aspects of your life could benefit from a "cleansing" similar to the metaphysical interpretation of the flood?

4. How do you relate to the concept of a "season for growth and transformation"? Is there a specific timeframe you could set for yourself to work on personal development?

5. Reflect on a time when you felt like the "floodwaters" had receded in your life. What were the signs that you were ready to move forward, similar to the dove returning in the Noah story?

Chapter Five
Tower of Babel

Introduction

The Tower of Babel story is a brief yet powerful narrative that addresses themes of hubris, unity, and the dispersion of human language and culture. Through a metaphysical lens, this chapter will explore the significance of collective ambition, the importance of divine alignment, and the intricacies of human communication.

Traditional Narrative

In the Book of Genesis, humans decide to build a tower that reaches the heavens to make a name for themselves and avoid being scattered across the Earth. Seeing this, God confuses their language and disperses them, making the completion of the tower impossible.

Biblical Context

The Tower of Babel is often interpreted as a cautionary tale against human arrogance and disobedience. It symbolically addresses the fragmentation of human communities and the limitations imposed by language and geographical dispersion.

Interfaith and Cultural Perspectives

Different traditions and myths also touch upon the hubris of humanity and the ensuing divine intervention. For example, the Greek myth of Icarus explores similar themes of overambition and the ensuing fall from grace.

Metaphysical Interpretation

According to Charles Fillmore's Metaphysical Bible Dictionary, the Tower of Babel symbolizes human ego and intellectual constructs aiming for divinity but not aligned with spiritual truth. The scattering and confusion of languages represent the disarray that follows when actions aren't rooted in higher consciousness.

Quotes and References

Fillmore suggests, "Whenever man attempts to accomplish anything without the aid of Spirit, he finds his language (expressive vehicles) confused." This idea highlights the necessity of spiritual alignment in our endeavors, whether individual or collective.

Real-world Examples

In today's world, projects driven by ego or material gain, without a spiritual or ethical foundation, often lead to discord or failure. On the other hand, endeavors rooted in higher values tend to unify people across diverse backgrounds.

Practical Applications

Before undertaking significant projects or life changes, consider aligning your intentions with higher spiritual principles. Techniques such as guided meditation or introspective journaling can help in attaining this alignment.

Reader Reflections

1. Have you ever been part of a project that failed due to misalignment or ego-driven motives? What lessons did you learn?
2. How do you interpret the notion of 'higher consciousness' or 'divine alignment' in your own life?

Concluding Thoughts

The story of the Tower of Babel, when viewed metaphysically, is not merely a cautionary tale but also an instructive narrative about the importance of divine alignment and the potential consequences of neglecting spiritual principles in our collective endeavors.

Glossary of Metaphysical Interpretations for This Chapter

- Tower of Babel: Symbol of ego-driven, unaligned human endeavors.
- Confusion of Languages: Disarray caused by actions not rooted in higher consciousness.
- Scattering of People: Symbolic of the isolation or division that comes from actions lacking spiritual alignment.

Additional Exercises

1. A guided meditation focusing on discerning ego-driven ambitions from higher, spiritually aligned goals.
2. Journaling prompts to explore your own experiences of alignment or misalignment in past projects or life events.

Chapter Five

Railroads and Reveries Amidst the Cornfields

As the ethereal glow of the descending sun bathed the world in hues of amber and gold, Michael, Ellery, and Tillie embarked on a journey not measured by miles but through the depths of insights gleaned along a seemingly endless stretch of railroad tracks. Surrounded by towering cornfields, whispering secrets of seasons past and present, they wandered amidst the steel and timber pathways, every step echoing with the gentle serenity of the evening.

"This expansive stretch of land and rails before us," Michael began, with a reflective glance towards the horizon, "reminds me somewhat of the tale of the Tower of Babel."

Tillie, who found comfort in the simplicity of their walks and the complexity of their dialogues, inquired with curiosity, lacing her words, "Dad, how does a story of a tower and a divine scattering relate to our journey today?"

With a thoughtful smile, Michael drew upon Charles

Fillmore's metaphysical interpretations, inviting his daughters into a deeper understanding of this ancient narrative. "In the traditional account, the Tower of Babel represents humanity's collective attempt to reach the heavens, which subsequently led to their dispersion and the confounding of their language. Metaphysically, it can symbolize our often misguided endeavors to attain enlightenment or spiritual heights through external means and self-aggrandizement."

Balancing precariously yet gracefully on the rail, Ellery considered the symbolism, her rebellious spirit always seeking truth amidst the conventional. "So, the scattering of people and languages might symbolize the dispersion of our focus and understanding when we seek externally rather than turning inward for spiritual growth?"

"Precisely, Ellery," Michael affirmed, admiring her depth of understanding. "And the multiplicity of languages can metaphysically represent the confusion and miscommunication that ensue when our ego drives our spiritual pursuits."

Pausing, he conveyed a thought from Henry David Thoreau that felt apt at that moment: "'It's not what you look at that matters, it's what you see.' Our individual spiritual paths are woven from our internal dialogues and insights, not from the external towers we construct in attempts to reach divinity."

As stones gently clicked against the metallic rails, thrown with contemplative precision by Tillie, the philosophical insights melded with the ambient sounds of the evening, crafting a web where reflections and memories intertwined.

Tillie, her artist's soul often finding meaning in metaphor, reflected aloud, "The tower, then, might symbolize illusions of our own making, and the scattering encourages us to dismantle unified but misguided external pursuits, directing us instead toward diverse, internal paths of spiritual understanding?"

Michael, his heart swelling with appreciation for the depth and beauty of his daughters' insights, nodded. "Indeed, Tillie. The story cautions us against seeking spiritual ascension through collective ego and material constructions. Instead, our paths, much like these diverging railroad tracks, guide us to explore the infinite landscapes within, each journey unique, yet intrinsically connected to the source of all creation."

Amidst the cornfields, under the slowly darkening sky, they continued their journey along the tracks, every step and shared reflection a testament to their individual and collective explorations of spiritual understanding. As the twilight gently enveloped the world around them, the fifth chapter of their exploration gently unfolded, into the next chapter of their story book. "Nailed it"

A Prayer

Dear Divine Wisdom,

Guide me as I navigate the projects and relationships that shape my life. Help me discern between endeavors fueled by ego and those inspired by a higher calling. May I strive not for towers of vanity but for bridges of understanding and compassion.

As I pursue my goals, let me remain aware of the spiritual principles that lend true meaning and purpose to my efforts. May my actions be rooted in higher consciousness, aligned with a deeper sense of unity and divine love.

When I encounter the inevitable 'Babel moments'—times of confusion, setbacks, or humility—may I see them as opportunities for reflection and realignment rather than failures?

Grant me the wisdom to recognize that true unity does not erase our differences but celebrates them in a collective endeavor aimed not at the heavens but at nurturing the divine spark within each human soul.

Amen.

Journaling Prompts

1. Reflect on a project or ambition in your life that didn't go as planned. Do you see any parallels with the Tower of Babel story? What might have been missing in terms of "divine alignment" or "higher consciousness"?

2. What does the term "spiritual alignment" mean to you personally? Can you identify a time when you felt you were in or out of spiritual alignment?

3. Consider a goal you have that may be considered "lofty" or ambitious. How could you approach it differently to ensure it is rooted in higher values or spiritual principles?

4. Think about your communication with others. Have you experienced moments of "confusion of languages," figuratively speaking, where misunderstandings arose? What could have been the underlying cause?

5. If the Tower of Babel symbolizes ego-driven endeavors, identify any projects or relationships in your life that may be fueled more by ego than by aligned purpose. What steps could you take to shift this?

Chapter Six
Abraham and Isaac

Introduction

The story of Abraham and Isaac is one of the most emotionally charged narratives in the Bible. Often interpreted as a tale of faith and obedience, its metaphysical reading offers deeper insights into the nature of sacrifice, transformation, and the inner conflicts we all face.

Traditional Narrative

God commands Abraham to sacrifice his son, Isaac, as a test of his faith. Just as Abraham is about to carry out the act, an angel intervenes, providing a ram as a substitute sacrifice. Abraham's faith is affirmed, and God blesses him abundantly.

Biblical Context

This story is critical in understanding the Judeo-Christian concept of faith. It has been variously interpreted, from a straightforward test of obedience to an allegory of divine sacrifice, particularly in Christian theology.

Interfaith and Cultural Perspectives

In Islamic tradition, the story is similar but usually identifies the son as Ishmael. The narrative serves as the basis for the Islamic holiday of Eid al-Adha, the Festival of Sacrifice.

Metaphysical Interpretation

Using Charles Fillmore's Metaphysical Bible Dictionary, Abraham represents the awakening of spiritual consciousness in humanity, while Isaac symbolizes the joy and vitality that come from spiritual realization. The story illustrates the inner conflict between our human desires and our quest for higher consciousness.

Quotes and References

Fillmore states, "The offering up of Isaac symbolizes the surrender of the personal for the impersonal." In this view, the story demonstrates the ultimate sacrifice: giving up what we most cherish for a greater spiritual good.

Real-world Examples

The internal struggle to align our actions with higher principles is a common human experience. This can manifest in making difficult ethical choices or surrendering short-term gratification for long-term well-being.

Practical Applications

Mindfulness and meditation practices can help us identify our 'Isaacs'—those things we hold dear but may need to surrender for higher spiritual growth. Consciously choosing principles over personal desires can be empowering.

Reader Reflections

1. Have you ever faced a situation where you had to sacrifice something dear to you for a higher cause?
2. How do you navigate the balance between personal desires and broader ethical or spiritual principles?

Concluding Thoughts

The story of Abraham and Isaac is a compelling narrative about the complexities of faith and the sacrifices required for spiritual growth. Through metaphysical interpretation, we find a framework for understanding our inner conflicts and for striving toward a higher state of being.

Glossary of Metaphysical Interpretations for This Chapter

- Abraham: Awakening spiritual consciousness
- Isaac: Joy and vitality stemming from spiritual realization
- Angel: Divine intervention or insight
- Ram: Substitute forms of sacrifice or dedication

Additional Exercises

1. Guided meditation to explore your values and potential areas of 'sacrifice' for spiritual or ethical growth.
2. Journaling prompts to evaluate instances where you've successfully or unsuccessfully navigated inner conflicts.

Chapter Six

Dawn Drives and Divine Dialogues

In the tranquil transition from the depths of the night to the soft light of an approaching dawn, Michael and his daughters, Ellery and Tillie, were embraced by the serene barrenness of the local back roads. Fields, emptied after the harvest, stretched boundlessly, offering a serene desolation beneath a gently illuminating sky.

The soothing hum of the car, journeying through the winding roads, provided a gentle melody in harmony with the distant murmur of waking wildlife. Michael gently introduced an ancient yet ever-pertinent narrative.

"This serene morning drive," Michael began, his voice a calm presence amidst the whispering wilderness, "reminds me of the story of Abraham and Isaac, a tale that unfolds deep metaphysical meanings when viewed through Fillmore's philosophical lens."

Tillie, her eyes reflecting the gentle colors of dawn, inquired, "What's the metaphysical understanding of that story, Dad?"

Michael delved into the explanation, "Abraham, asked by God to sacrifice his son, Isaac, is metaphorically a tale where Abraham symbolizes the will, and Isaac represents joy or the potential for good. The willingness to sacrifice Isaac symbolizes the surrender of personal joy or desire to a higher divine will."

Ellery, whose rebellious spark had matured into a thoughtful flame, mused, "So, it's not actually about a physical sacrifice, but more an internal surrender of our personal wants in alignment with something higher and spiritual?"

"Exactly, Ellery," Michael affirmed, his eyes navigating between the unfolding path ahead and his daughters beside him. "This internal surrender doesn't obliterate our joys or desires. Instead, it refines them, aligning our personal will with the divine, which invariably enhances our joy and fulfillment."

As they glided through the serene emptiness of the harvested fields, with dawn's light gently awakening the world, Michael thoughtfully shared the words of philosopher Albert Camus: "Real generosity towards the future lies in giving all to the present."

Silence embraced the trio as they journeyed through the awakening day, pondering the depths of the allegory, seeking connections between ancient stories and their present paths. Perennial wisdom woven through time, inviting understanding and spiritual unfoldment, accompanied their continuing journey - both the immediate voyage along uncharted paths and the profound internal exploration, each mile and metaphor guiding them towards unexplored territories of comprehension and spiritual development.

A Prayer

Dear Divine Guide,

As I walk the challenging path of ethical and spiritual choices, grant me the wisdom to discern the higher principles that should guide my actions. Help me to recognize my own 'Isaacs'—those precious aspects of life that I hold dear but may need to surrender for the greater good.

In times of moral dilemma, may I find the courage to prioritize long-term spiritual growth over short-term comfort or gain. Should I face tests of my faith or convictions, strengthen me to stand firm and remain aligned with my deepest values?

If I am granted a 'ram in the thicket,' a sudden reprieve from tough decisions, let me take it as a sign of your guiding presence. May such moments deepen my faith and help me grow into a person who reflects your love, wisdom, and compassion.

In every trial, let me emerge not just with solutions but with greater understanding and spiritual depth, for it is through navigating life's intricate ethical and spiritual landscape that I come closer to you.

Amen.

Journaling Prompts

1. Reflect on a time when you faced an ethical or moral dilemma. What were the conflicting values, and how did you resolve them?

2. In your life, what or who represents your 'Isaac'—something precious that you might need to surrender for a higher cause? How does the thought of letting go make you feel?

3. The story of Abraham and Isaac talks about the testing of faith. Have you ever felt your own faith or principles were being tested? How did you respond?

4. Think about the concept of 'substitute sacrifice,' as represented by the ram in the biblical story. Have you experienced a moment when an alternative solution appeared, sparing you from making a difficult choice?

5. According to Fillmore, Abraham represents awakening spiritual consciousness. Identify a situation where you felt your spiritual consciousness was awakened or deepened. What prompted this shift?

Chapter Seven
Jacob and Esau

Introduction

The narrative of Jacob and Esau delves into themes of rivalry, identity, and transformation. While it's often read as a cautionary tale about deceit and family discord, a metaphysical interpretation allows us to see it as a story about the struggle between our lower and higher selves.

Traditional Narrative

Jacob and Esau are twins, with Esau being the elder. Jacob deceives his father, Isaac, to receive the blessing intended for Esau, resulting in estrangement between the brothers. After years of separation and personal transformation, they eventually reconcile.

Biblical Context

This story is one of the foundational narratives of the Hebrew Bible, reflecting issues like inheritance rights, the complexities of family relationships, and the consequences of deceit.

Interfaith and Cultural Perspectives

The tale is significant in both Jewish and Christian traditions, often symbolizing the spiritual journey. Islamic tradition also includes the story, emphasizing the moral lessons to be drawn from the siblings' actions.

Metaphysical Interpretation

According to Charles Fillmore's Metaphysical Bible Dictionary, Jacob represents the intellectual or cunning aspect of human consciousness, while Esau symbolizes the more primal or instinctual side. The story illustrates the conflict and eventual harmonization of these two aspects of ourselves.

Quotes and References

Fillmore writes, "Esau symbolizes the body consciousness, which is first in expression but not in importance." This perspective helps us understand why the "younger" (Jacob) eventually gains prominence over the "older" (Esau) in the narrative.

Real-world Examples

We all face moments where we must choose between

immediate gratification (Esau) and long-term well-being or wisdom (Jacob). Over time, a balanced integration often leads to personal growth and more harmonious relationships.

Practical Applications

Practices like mindfulness can help us recognize when we are acting out of primal instincts versus when we are making choices aligned with higher wisdom. The aim is to bring these two aspects into harmony.

Reader Reflections

1. Can you identify moments in your life when you faced a Jacob-Esau type of dilemma?
2. How do you aim to harmonize your instinctual and intellectual sides?

Concluding Thoughts

The story of Jacob and Esau provides a rich understanding our inner complexities. Through a metaphysical lens, it serves as an allegory for personal growth, highlighting the importance of integrating various aspects of our consciousness.

Glossary of Metaphysical Interpretations for This Chapter

- Jacob: Intellectual or cunning aspect of human consciousness
- Esau: Primal or instinctual aspect of human consciousness
- Blessing: Symbolizes the acknowledgment or enhancement of one's higher faculties.

Additional Exercises

1. A guided meditation focusing on identifying and harmonizing your 'Jacob' and 'Esau' aspects.
2. Journaling prompts that help you examine past experiences where these two aspects were in conflict and how you resolved them.

Chapter Seven

Pizza and Parables in December Evenings

The soft hum of the evening settled around the kitchen, mingling with the scent of Mimo's pizza that wafted through the air. The dim glow of the overhead lights cast a warm ambiance throughout the space. Michael leaned against the kitchen counter, savoring the zesty aroma of the pizza after a long day of welding, the fatigue evident in his posture but his eyes shining with a steadfast vigor.

Ellery and Tillie, seated comfortably on the island, greeted their father with welcoming eyes and warm smiles. The boxes of pizza popped open to reveal their delightful contents, promising a soothing comfort that only familiar flavors could provide.

"We've got your favorite, Dad," Tillie mentioned, nudging a box slightly toward him.

"Much appreciated, Tills," Michael acknowledged, gently lifting a slice, the cheese stringing along in melty tendrils.

As they indulged in their dinner, the warm familiarity of the cheesy slices in their hands, an age-old story found its way into their conversation.

"Girls," Michael began, his voice carrying a thoughtful tremor, "Do you remember the story of Jacob and Esau from the Bible?"

Ellery, ever the contemplative one, responded, "The twins? Jacob tricked Esau into giving up his birthright and blessing, right?"

"That's correct," Michael confirmed, taking a deliberate bite of his pizza before continuing. "In Charles Fillmore's metaphysical interpretation, Jacob and Esau represent two fundamental aspects within us. Esau symbolizes the physical, material consciousness, while Jacob represents the intellectual and more spiritually attuned aspect."

The daughters listened intently, bites of pizza pausing midway to their mouths as their father continued.

"Esau was the firstborn, and thus, initially, our material desires and physicality often take precedence. But as we grow and evolve, the 'Jacob' within us seeks something deeper, seeking to supersede mere physical wants and connecting with our higher spiritual selves."

He took a sip of his beer, the bubbles softly fizzing, and

allowed the silence to linger for a moment.

Ellery leaned forward, "So, in a way, it's about our inner journey from being materially driven to seeking a deeper spiritual understanding?"

Michael nodded, "Very much so, Ellery. It's not about deceiving others but transcending our own internal material limitations to tap into a higher understanding, just as Jacob did by acquiring the birthright and blessing."

Tillie, her mind painting the words into internal imagery, spoke up, "It's kind of beautiful how ancient stories can reflect our internal struggles and journeys."

Indeed, this contemplation brought a philosophical depth to their gathering around the kitchen island. With pizza slices mid-air and the subtle fizz of Michael's beer punctuating their dialogue, a quote emanated from his memory.

Quoting Neville Goddard, Michael offered, "Assume the feeling of your wish fulfilled and observe the route that your attention follows."

A contemplative silence followed, broken only by the occasional crunch of the crust. Each one, in its own rhythm, mulled over the layers of metaphysical understanding encapsulated in the biblical tale.

Their dialogue continued, navigating through layers of interpretations, stories, and metaphysical philosophies, all within the comforting familiarity of their kitchen. The simple act of sharing pizza had transformed into an intimate communion of minds and spirits, exploring the boundaries of material and spiritual realms.

In that shared space, amidst the aroma of Mimo's pizza and under the soft glow of the overhead lights, ancient parables found a modern echo, gently guiding them through metaphysical explorations. Together, they discovered that within the mundane, the sacred often finds a dwelling place, unfolding profound truths amidst the simplest acts of daily living.

Their exploration of ancient tales, philosophically rich dialogues, and the shared simplicity of a pizza dinner subtly highlighted the sacred within the every day - embodying, indeed, that in understanding and communion, every moment, every meal, and every dialogue could transcend into something profoundly spiritual. And there, amidst cheese and crust, spiritual and material, the ancient and the modern dialogue, finding unity in their shared moment in time.

A Prayer

Dear Divine Source,

Guide me through the inner landscapes of my consciousness, where the cunning intellect of Jacob and the raw instinct of Esau often clash. Grant me the wisdom to recognize when each aspect has its role to play and the strength to bring them into harmony.

As I face life's choices, big and small, it helps me to act with moral integrity and never lose sight of my higher self. When I falter or err, may I find the courage to seek reconciliation, both with others and within myself.

Like the twins in their later years, let me grow from my experiences, finding reconciliation and harmony. May my journey be not just a series of choices but a path toward greater self-awareness and self-acceptance.

For in balancing the diverse facets of my being, I draw closer to the harmonious whole you intend for me to be.

Amen.

Journaling Prompts

1. Reflect on a time when you felt a tug-of-war between your intellectual side (Jacob) and your instinctual side (Esau). What was the situation, and how did you navigate it?

2. Can you think of a relationship where a 'Jacob-Esau' dynamic was present? How did that relationship evolve over time, and were there any significant moments of reconciliation or understanding?

3. Identify instances where your strategic planning (Jacob) and hands-on capabilities (Esau) harmonized to create something greater. How did this synergy feel?

4. Fillmore suggests that Esau represents the body consciousness, which is "first in expression but not in importance." Have you had moments where you prioritized physical or immediate desires only to later realize the importance of intellectual or ethical considerations?

Chapter Eight
Joseph and His Coat of Many Colors

Introduction

The story of Joseph and his coat of many colors captures our imagination with themes of dreams, jealousy, betrayal, and eventual redemption. Metaphysically, it serves as a multi-layered narrative about the richness of human experience, personal growth, and the transformative power of forgiveness.

Traditional Narrative

Joseph, the favored son of Jacob, receives a coat of many colors from his father. His brothers, envious of this favoritism and Joseph's prophetic dreams, sell him into slavery. He rises to power in Egypt, eventually reconciling with his brothers during a famine.

Biblical Context

This account is pivotal in the Hebrew Bible for setting the stage for the Israelites' eventual move to Egypt, which leads to their enslavement and the Exodus story.

Interfaith and Cultural Perspectives

The narrative is also present in the Islamic tradition. In Christianity, Joseph is often seen as a type of Christ figure, suffering unjustly but ultimately forgiving and redeeming his persecutors.

Metaphysical Interpretation

Drawing upon Charles Fillmore's Metaphysical Bible Dictionary, Joseph symbolizes the human capacity for divine imagination or vision. The coat of many colors represents the diversity and richness of our spiritual faculties, including intuition, wisdom, and understanding.

Quotes and References

Fillmore mentions, "The coat of many colors symbolizes the many faculties that are developed under spiritual understanding." Through this lens, Joseph's story is a journey toward actualizing these faculties, even amidst adversity.

Real-world Examples

Think of people who have turned significant setbacks into opportunities for growth. Often, it's their vision, resilience, and the 'richness' of their character that allows them to transform circumstances.

Practical Applications

Mindfulness and visualization exercises can help you tune into your 'Joseph-like' faculties. The focus is on strengthening your inner vision and resilience to handle life's challenges effectively.

Reader Reflections

1. Have you ever had a 'coat of many colors' moment where your unique abilities or insights were both a blessing and a source of conflict?
2. How do you cope with adversity, and what 'colors' do you rely on to navigate through challenges?

Concluding Thoughts

Joseph's story serves as a rich allegory about the complexities and paradoxes of human existence. Metaphysically, it offers a roadmap for personal and spiritual growth, highlighting the transformative power of adversity when approached with vision and resilience.

Glossary of Metaphysical Interpretations for This Chapter

- Joseph: Human capacity for divine imagination or vision
- Coat of Many Colors: Diversity and richness of spiritual faculties
- Dreams: Intuitive messages or goals
- Famine: Spiritual or emotional lack

Additional Exercises

1. A guided meditation to explore your own 'coat of many colors'—your diverse spiritual and emotional faculties.
2. Journaling prompts that encourage reflection on your own life journeys that parallel Joseph's story.

Chapter Eight
Swings and Multicolored Musings

On the quaint porch of Michael's mother's house, the gentle sway of the swing sang an unobtrusive melody, accompanying the casual yet profound conversation. Michael, seated, was carefully crafting a grape blunt, the rich aroma of weed permeating the soft, ambient air. Ellery, with her vibrant and rebellious spirit, sat beside, while Tillie, fresh from school and soon to be ensnared by the demands of her job, joined them, her demeanor calm yet mildly encumbered by the awaiting evening shift.

The sun, now dipped beneath the horizon, cast the world into a serene twilight; as Michael finally allowed the lighter's flame to kiss the blunt, he put it to his lips, inhaling deeply.

In the midst of their tranquil yet somewhat bittersweet gathering, Michael, exhaling a thoughtful cloud, began, "You know, there's a story in the Bible about a young man named Joseph. He was gifted a coat of many colors by his father, which stirred jealousy and resentment among his brothers."

The girls leaned in, the familiar cadence of a story to be told gently pulling them into the narrative.

He continued, "Joseph, amidst betrayals and hardship, never lost his unwavering faith and integrity. He endured, transforming his misfortunes into opportunities, rising to great prominence despite the adversity thrust upon him."

Ellery questioned, "So it's a tale of persistence and faith amidst adversity?"

"Indeed," Michael responded, taking another gentle pull. "Joseph represents the dreamer within us, and his multicolored coat symbolizes the vibrant, dream-like spiritual consciousness, according to Charles Fillmore. Despite being enshrouded by the darkness of jealousy, betrayal, and challenge, that vivid, internal spiritual consciousness remains untouched and potent."

Tillie, ever the observer, traced her fingers along the chain of the swing, contributing, "There's something universally relatable about it – facing adversities, being misunderstood, and yet maintaining one's integrity and hope."

A genuine smile appeared upon Michael's lips, appreciating the insightful pondering emerging amidst the haze and swing's gentle sway.

Softly, he shared a quote from Leo Tolstoy, "Just as one candle lights another and can light thousands of other candles, so one heart illuminates another heart and can illuminate thousands of other hearts."

It lingered in the air, intertwining with the fading plumes of smoke, inviting a moment of contemplative silence among them.

Tillie glanced at her phone, the impending responsibility of work casting a mild shadow upon her youthful expression, yet within her eyes, a flicker of fortified resolve gleamed.

Ellery, ever empathetic, placed a gentle hand upon Tillie's, whispering reassurances of brighter tomorrows and dreams yet to unfold.

And so, there on the porch swing, they found a sacred space where biblical parables and metaphysical insights wove a web rich with understanding, camaraderie, and a shared light that, even amidst the encroaching night, promised to illuminate their paths in profound and unexpected ways.

A Prayer

Dear Divine Source,

Bless me with the vision to see the colorful fabric that is my inner self, woven from threads of intuition, wisdom, and understanding. Help me to embrace the full spectrum of my faculties, even when others may not understand or appreciate them.

When I face setbacks, betrayals, or the 'famine of the soul,' may I draw upon my inner richness to find resilience and growth. Let my adversities be the loom upon which a more intricate and colorful self is woven.

Grant me the wisdom to recognize the transformative power of forgiveness, not just for those who have wronged me but also for myself. As I navigate the complexities of human relationships and personal growth, guide me toward a life filled with grace, resilience, and a wealth of spiritual faculties.

Amen.

Journaling Prompts

1. Identify your own 'coat of many colors'—the range of spiritual faculties, skills, or talents you possess. How have you used these faculties to navigate challenges or to help others?

2. Farid mentions that Joseph's life is a testament to enduring patience and divine providence. Can you think of an instance where patience and faith guided you through a difficult time?

3. Considering Fillmore's metaphysical interpretation, have you ever felt like your inner richness was attacked or undermined? How did you respond, and what did it reveal about your character?

Chapter Nine
Moses and the Exodus

Introduction

The story of Moses and the Exodus is a seminal tale of liberation and leadership. While traditionally viewed as a historical account of the Israelites' escape from Egyptian slavery, a metaphysical interpretation offers insights into personal and spiritual freedom.

Traditional Narrative

Born to an Israelite family but raised in Pharaoh's court, Moses flees Egypt after killing an Egyptian taskmaster. He encounters God in a burning bush and returns to lead the Israelites out of slavery, parting the Red Sea and receiving the Ten Commandments on Mount Sinai.

Biblical Context

The Exodus is a foundational story in Judaism and significantly influences Christian and Islamic teachings. It outlines the formation of Israelite identity and their covenant with God.

Interfaith and Cultural Perspectives

The Exodus story is not only crucial in Abrahamic religions but also has parallels in other spiritual traditions where liberation from suffering or bondage is a central theme.

Metaphysical Interpretation

According to Charles Fillmore's Metaphysical Bible Dictionary, Moses represents the law of divine justice and order. The Israelites symbolize different aspects of human consciousness seeking liberation, and Egypt represents material bondage or ignorance.

Quotes and References

Fillmore states, "Moses typifies that in us which discerns the right when it is presented." The burning bush is seen as an awakening of spiritual consciousness, illuminating the path toward freedom.

Real-world Examples

Anyone striving for personal freedom—whether from toxic relationships, bad habits, or limiting beliefs—can relate to the Exodus story. Liberation often comes when we heed our inner

'Moses'—the voice of reason and justice.

Practical Applications

Reflective practices can help you identify your own 'Egypt'—areas in life where you feel trapped. Mindfulness and ethical principles serve as your 'Moses,' guiding you toward liberation.

Reader Reflections

1. What are your personal 'Egypts' or areas where you feel confined?

2. How do you listen to your inner 'Moses,' and what steps have you taken toward liberation?

Concluding Thoughts

The story of Moses and the Exodus is rich with metaphysical symbolism, offering a roadmap for personal and spiritual liberation. By understanding these deeper meanings, we can apply its lessons to achieve greater freedom in our own lives.

Glossary of Metaphysical Interpretations for This Chapter

- Moses: Law of divine justice and order

- Israelites: Different aspects of human consciousness
- Egypt: Material bondage or ignorance
- Burning Bush: Awakening of spiritual consciousness
- Red Sea: Emotional obstacles
- Ten Commandments: Fundamental spiritual principles

Additional Exercises

1. Guided meditation to focus on your 'burning bush moments,' instances where clarity and purpose were suddenly illuminated.
2. Journaling prompts that help you outline your own Exodus journey, from recognizing bondage to achieving freedom.

Chapter Nine
December Drive with Moses

The world outside was laced with a delicate frost, each blade of grass encased in a fragile sheen, glistening as the dawn light gently caressed the frozen landscape. In the distance, herds of deer grazed peacefully in the barren fields, their warm breaths painting ephemeral clouds in the crisp winter air.

Inside the car, a warm, comforting atmosphere enveloped Michael and his daughters, Tillie and Ellery, as they meandered through the countryside, sipping quietly on their coffees.

Michael, glancing appreciatively at the serene vistas outside, began to weave a tale into the peaceful ambiance of the car, "Moses, as you might remember, led his people, the Israelites, from the harsh servitude in Egypt towards a promised land flowing with milk and honey. It's a journey fraught with challenges, despair, faith, and miracles."

As the vehicle hummed smoothly along the frosty roads, the girls listened intently, the biblical narrative intermingling with their own thoughts and the serene landscapes unfolding before their eyes.

He continued, "This Exodus wasn't just a physical journey, but also, in the lens of metaphysics and Charles Fillmore's perspective, it's a symbolic one. The departure from Egypt symbolizes our own journey from a state of mental and spiritual bondage toward a promise of enlightenment and peace. Egypt signifies the dark recesses of our mind, enslaved by material and oppressive thoughts, while the Promised Land represents a state of spiritual fulfillment and abundance."

Ellery, her reflection faintly visible on the window beside her, queried, "So, it's like an internal struggle and journey we all go through? A quest towards our own spiritual and mental liberation?"

"Exactly, E," Michael affirmed, "Moses, in this metaphysical lens, represents the directive power of the mind, that which commands our thoughts and actions, leading us from the shadowy depths of ignorance and materialism toward spiritual insight and light."

Tillie, gently holding the warm exterior of her coffee cup, chimed in, "But the journey isn't straightforward, is it? Just like the Israelites encountered numerous challenges, our path towards inner peace and understanding is often mired with its own struggles and moments of despair."

"You're quite right, Tillie," Michael responded thoughtfully, "the path is never linear. And it's in those moments of struggle and despair where our truest growth often happens. It's about embracing the journey, with its trials, revelations, and its moments of difficulties."

He shared a quote from Alan Watts, hoping to tether the biblical narrative to a philosophical strand, "The only way to make sense out of change is to plunge into it, move with it, and join the dance."

As they drove through the quiet December morning, the philosophical and biblical nuances settled around them like a gentle snowfall, each flake a thought, a contemplation, sparking introspective fires and nurturing the ever-unfolding journey within. With Moses' journey echoing in their minds, they meandered through the frosted landscapes, finding a tranquil alignment between the ancient tales of exodus and their own ever-evolving narratives.

A Prayer

Dear Divine Wisdom,

Grant me the discernment to recognize my own 'Egypts'—the areas of confinement and ignorance that hold me back. May I awaken to my personal 'burning bush moments,' those flashes of spiritual and moral clarity that light the path toward freedom.

Let me embody the spirit of Moses within, the inner law of divine justice and order, as I navigate the complexities of life. Help me to unite the various aspects of my consciousness in a common quest for liberation, breaking the chains of material bondage.

In facing my Red Sea moments, arm me with courage and insight to part the waters of emotional obstacles. And as I journey towards my own promised land, may I not forget to lay down my Ten Commandments—principles that guide not just me but those whose lives I touch.

Amen.

Journaling Prompts

1. Consider your own "burning bush moments"—instances where you felt an undeniable call to action or a sudden clarity of purpose. What ignited these moments, and how did they change you?

2. Have you faced emotional obstacles that felt insurmountable? How did you overcome them, and what or who guided you through?

3. Like the Israelites represent different aspects of human consciousness. What aspects of your own consciousness do you need to unite to achieve personal liberation?

4. "Ten Commandments." What would your own Ten Commandments of life be—fundamental principles that guide your moral and ethical decisions?

Chapter Ten
The Ten Commandments

Introduction

The Ten Commandments serve as a moral and ethical code that has influenced various facets of law, ethics, and morality in the Western world. Beyond their traditional understanding, a metaphysical approach provides a unique lens to explore these ancient laws as principles for spiritual and personal growth.

Traditional Narrative

After the Exodus from Egypt, Moses ascends Mount Sinai, where he receives the Ten Commandments from God. These laws are meant to govern the Israelites' behavior and solidify their covenant with God.

Biblical Context

The Ten Commandments have a foundational role in Judaism and have also been integrated into Christian ethics. They are often viewed as universal moral principles.

Interfaith and Cultural Perspectives

Besides Judaism and Christianity, aspects of the Commandments can be found in other ethical systems and religious traditions, though the interpretations may differ.

Metaphysical Interpretation

According to Charles Fillmore's Metaphysical Bible Dictionary, the Ten Commandments can be viewed as fundamental spiritual laws that govern human consciousness. For example, "Thou shalt not kill" can be extended to mean the eradication of negative thoughts or emotions.

Quotes and References

Fillmore notes, "The Commandments represent a code of 'mental conduct' that, when obeyed, helps to bring the individual into harmony with divine law."

Real-world Examples

The principle of not bearing false witness, for instance, can be applied to our current 'fake news' era, where integrity in communication is crucial for societal harmony.

Practical Applications

Reflect on how each Commandment can be translated into a guiding principle in your daily life. For example, honoring one's parents can extend to respecting all forms of guidance and wisdom.

Reader Reflections

1. Which Commandment do you find most relevant to your current life situation?
2. How can you apply the metaphysical interpretation of the Commandments to your daily experiences?

Concluding Thoughts

The Ten Commandments, when viewed metaphysically, offer more than just a set of rules; they provide a framework for personal and spiritual development, allowing us to live in greater harmony with ourselves and the world around us.

Glossary of Metaphysical Interpretations for This Chapter

- Ten Commandments: Fundamental spiritual laws governing human consciousness
- Mount Sinai: A symbol of elevated consciousness or spiritual enlightenment

- Covenant: A spiritual agreement or bond between the individual and the Divine

Additional Exercises

1. A guided meditation focusing on one Commandment at a time, exploring its deeper metaphysical meaning.
2. Journaling exercises to contemplate how each Commandment can become a practical guide in your life.

Chapter Ten

Icebound Reflections on the Commandments

The chill of January hung heavily in the air as Michael, Ellery, and Tillie gingerly made their way across the frozen expanse of the lake. Their boots crunched and squeaked upon the thick, resilient ice, every step an interplay between awe and cautious respect for nature's precarious beauty.

Beneath the solid surface, bubbles were suspended in stasis, providing a curious lens through which to ponder the world beneath and the sky above. Michael crouched down, his hands deftly moving to clear a patch of ice, revealing the dormant, yet vibrant, life underneath.

His voice, calm and introspective, mingled with the frosty air, "The tale of Moses and the Ten Commandments offers layers of depth when looked at metaphysically. It's not merely about an ancient leader providing divine laws to his people, but also about our own internal moral compass, directing our journey through life."

Ellery, lying on the ice, gazed into the clear window to the watery world below, her breath creating transient clouds upon the surface, "Dad, this idea of a moral compass, do you think it's inherent or something society and experiences shape within us?"

Michael pondered, "I think it's a bit of both, Ellery. We all possess a certain innate moral sense, yet it's continuously molded by our experiences and interactions. The Ten Commandments, in this light, can be seen not just as stringent laws, but as guiding principles, enabling harmony within and without."

Tillie, her fingers tracing the trapped bubbles beneath the ice, voiced, "So, it's like they serve as a framework that helps us navigate through life, to coexist harmoniously with others, and to find a balance in our own internal dichotomies?"

"Precisely, Tillie," Michael affirmed. He breathed deeply,

the crisp air filling his lungs, before reciting a quote from Leo Tolstoy, "'Wrong does not cease to be wrong because the majority share in it.' This reflection kindles the thought that the commandments, or our internal moral codes, serve to anchor us amidst the diverse tides of societal norms and pressures."

Lying beside Ellery, looking deeply into the ice as if hoping to discern hidden truths in its depths, Michael shared, "Moses might symbolize our inner guide or the voice of our higher self, conveying those essential truths or commandments that guide us toward a life of integrity and genuine connection with the Divine."

Ellery, peering at the vegetation below the ice, mused, "And it's a constant journey, isn't it? To listen to that inner Moses, to be led by those moral and spiritual imperatives, especially when external chaos or challenges ensue."

As they lay there, gazing into the ethereal underwater world suspended beneath them, tranquility enveloped them, the philosophical musings intertwining with the Biblical narratives, forging a connection that transcended time and space.

In that serene, frozen moment, amidst conversations of moral compasses and spiritual journeys, Michael and his daughters found a peaceful confluence of the ancient and the present, the metaphysical and the tangible, all upon a fragile yet enduring sheet of ice.

A Prayer

Divine Wisdom,

As I seek to climb my own Mount Sinai of elevated consciousness, I humbly ask for the insight to perceive the deeper truths within the Ten Commandments. May they serve as guiding stars on my journey towards personal and spiritual growth.

Grant me the strength to face my limitations, the wisdom to understand the universality of these ancient laws, and the clarity to apply them in a way that enriches not just my life but also the lives of those around me.

Let me honor these Commandments not as mere obligations but as a spiritual toolkit that aids me in navigating life's complexities. May they lead me from Egypt of my own limitations to the promised land of higher consciousness and deeper understanding.

Amen.

Chapter Ten: The Ten Commandments

Journaling Prompts

1. Which Commandment do you think most directly applies to your current emotional or mental state, and why?

2. Choose one Commandment and meditate on its deeper, metaphysical meaning. How does this change your perspective on its relevance to your life?

3. The Fourth Commandment, "Remember the Sabbath day," sparks a conversation about work-life balance. How well do you maintain this balance, and what steps could you take to honor your own "Sabbath" moments for rest and reflection?

4. Which Commandment would you pick as your personal challenge, and how would you go about embodying it for a week?

Chapter Eleven
Joshua and the Battle of Jericho

Introduction

The story of Joshua and the Battle of Jericho serves as a profound example of faith and obedience leading to miraculous outcomes. In a metaphysical context, it can be seen as an allegory for overcoming seemingly insurmountable obstacles in our personal and spiritual lives.

Traditional Narrative

After Moses' death, Joshua leads the Israelites into Canaan. With divine guidance, the Israelites marched around the fortified city of Jericho for seven days. On the seventh day, the walls of the city collapse, and they conquer it.

Biblical Context

The Battle of Jericho marks the Israelites' first conquest of Canaan, the land promised to them by God. It sets the tone for their future endeavors in establishing a homeland.

Interfaith and Cultural Perspectives

While primarily a Jewish and Christian tale, the story is also acknowledged in Islamic tradition. It serves as a lesson in unwavering faith across these religious contexts.

Metaphysical Interpretation

According to Charles Fillmore's Metaphysical Bible Dictionary, Joshua represents the "I AM" identity in humans that can realize and act on divine guidance. Jericho symbolizes a mental stronghold that can be overcome through spiritual understanding and faith.

Quotes and References

Fillmore remarks, "Joshua symbolizes that in us which is established in the good and true." This essence helps us overcome mental 'walls' that confine us.

Real-world Examples

Think of instances where your faith or conviction helped you overcome a seemingly impossible situation. These are your personal 'Jericho moments.'

Practical Applications

Mindfulness practices can help identify your own 'Jerichos'—those mental or emotional walls that seem hard to break down. Exercises in faith and positive affirmation can be your metaphorical seven days of circling.

Reader Reflections

1. What are the 'walls of Jericho' in your life that you find difficult to break down?
2. How can faith or conviction aid you in overcoming these barriers?

Concluding Thoughts

The story of Joshua and the Battle of Jericho serves as a metaphysical blueprint for overcoming obstacles through faith and divine guidance. When we align ourselves with spiritual principles, the impossible becomes attainable.

Glossary of Metaphysical Interpretations for This Chapter

- Joshua: "I AM" identity realizing and acting on divine guidance
- Jericho: Mental stronghold overcome through spiritual

understanding

- Seven Days: Symbolizes completion or divine timing
- Canaan: Representing the 'Promised Land' or a state of spiritual fulfillment

Additional Exercises

1. A guided meditation on identifying and 'circling' your own walls, focusing on how faith can bring them down.
2. Journaling prompts to explore your personal 'Jericho moments' and the role of faith in your life.

Chapter Eleven
Echoes in the Cemetery – Joshua and the Battle of Jericho

Snow blanketed the quiet, old cemetery as Michael, Ellery, and Tillie tread softly between the weathered gravestones. The inscriptions, eroded by time, whispered tales from the 1800s, their stories veiled by the relentless passage of years. Surrounded by an encircling embrace of leafless woods and with a clear, starlit sky overhead, the atmosphere was serene yet tinged with poignant reminiscence.

"Each one of these stones tells a story," Michael began, "a tale of a life lived, of joys and sorrows, victories and defeats." His breath formed a small cloud in the cold January air.

Tillie, rubbing her hands together for warmth, mused aloud, "It's kind of sad but beautiful too. All these people had lives as vivid and complex as ours, and now all that's left are these markers, frozen in time."

Ellery, pulling her scarf tighter, nodded, "And in many ways, they continue to live on – through us. Our existence is interwoven with theirs."

Michael smiled, guiding the conversation toward their next biblical exploration. "Speaking of tales and history, today's story is one of battle and faith: Joshua and the Battle of Jericho."

He paused, ensuring he had the captivation of his daughters, then delved into the story, "Joshua, leading the Israelites, was tasked with conquering Jericho, a seemingly impregnable city protected by formidable walls. They were guided not by strategies of war but by the unusual instructions from God: to march around the city for six days and, on the seventh day, to encircle it seven times, culminating with a grand, resonating trumpet blast."

Tillie, perching on a low stone wall, engaged, "I've always found that story curious. I mean, the idea of walls crumbling by merely walking around them and blowing trumpets, it's not something you find in any tactical war guide." She laughed.

Ellery chimed in, "But isn't that precisely the essence, Tillie? It wasn't about employing conventional warfare methods. It was a symbolic act demonstrating faith and obedience, a metaphor for our personal walls crumbling when we embrace trust and spiritual guidance."

A nod from Michael affirmed Ellery's perspective. "In Fillmore's metaphysical interpretation, Jericho represents the 'sense-consciousness,' which is often fortified, hindering the influx of spiritual insights. The walls symbolize our rigid beliefs or prejudices, and their collapse underlines the potential of faith to dismantle even the sturdiest barriers within us."

Tillie's brow furrowed thoughtfully, "So, in a way, we all have our Jerichos, walls we've built that keep us from fully embracing a higher consciousness or truth?"

"Yes, Tills, and navigating through or around them necessitates a form of surrender, an acknowledgment of a power beyond our intellectual understanding," Michael responded, his eyes reflecting the scattered moonlight upon the snow.

Bringing forth a quote to illuminate their discussion, he shared words from philosopher Alan Watts: "'To have faith is to trust yourself to the water. When you swim, you don't grab hold of the water because if you do, you will sink and drown. Instead, you relax and float.'"

The words lingered, intertwining with the silent stories of the departed encircling them. Ellery, looking up at the vast, endless night sky, whispered, "It's a ceaseless journey, isn't it? This constant, cyclical process of identifying and dismantling the walls we subconsciously erect."

Michael, his voice soft yet firm, concurred, "Indeed, Ellery. It is a perpetual pilgrimage toward awakening, breaking down barriers, and allowing the spirit to flow unimpeded."

In the quietude of the cemetery, amidst the tales of lives once lived, Michael and his daughters found a solemn sanctuary to reflect upon their internal landscapes. As they slowly walked back towards the car, the soft crunching of their footsteps in the snow keeping rhythm with their ponderings, they carried with them not just the echoes of ancient parables but reflections on their modern-day journey through the labyrinth of life and consciousness.

And so, under the celestial gaze of myriad stars, the trio recognizing that every wall encountered was but a call toward greater understanding and deeper faith in their story, "Nailed It."

A Prayer

Dear God (or the Divine Force you connect with),

I come to you burdened by the walls of my own Jericho—obstacles that appear formidable, both in my mind and in my life. I ask for the courage to face these walls, the strength to circle them, and the wisdom to bring them tumbling down.

Help me to embrace the "I AM" within me that I may realize and act upon Your divine guidance. As the Israelites found their Promised Land beyond the walls of Jericho, may I, too, find my own land of spiritual and personal fulfillment.

Grant me the faith to trust in Your timing and the resilience to continue marching, even when progress feels slow or absent.

In faith and courage, I pray, Amen.

Journaling Prompts

1. Reflect on a time when you had to step into a new role or responsibility. What fears or "walls" did you face, and how did you overcome them?

2. The story of Joshua and the Battle of Jericho is present in multiple religious traditions. Do you see the principles of faith and courage as universally applicable in your life, regardless of your religious or spiritual background? Why or why not?

3. How do you currently engage with your "I AM" identity, and in what ways could nurturing this aspect of yourself assist you in conquering your Jerichos?

Chapter Twelve
Judges - The Story of Samson

Introduction

The story of Samson from the Book of Judges is a compelling tale of strength, temptation, and redemption. Metaphysically, it explores the dynamics of personal power and the consequences of its misuse.

Traditional Narrative

Samson, a Nazirite endowed with superhuman strength, is betrayed by his love, Delilah, who reveals the secret of his power—his uncut hair—to the Philistines. Eventually blinded and imprisoned, he redeems himself by bringing down the Philistine temple.

Biblical Context

Samson's narrative serves as a cautionary tale about the misuse of divine gifts. It also explores the themes of temptation and redemption, common throughout the Bible.

Interfaith and Cultural Perspectives

While primarily significant in the Jewish and Christian traditions, the story of Samson has found its way into various forms of literature and folklore, emphasizing universal themes of strength and vulnerability.

Metaphysical Interpretation

According to Charles Fillmore's Metaphysical Bible Dictionary, Samson symbolizes the untamed spiritual strength that resides within each of us. His hair represents the outward expression of this inner power.

Quotes and References

Fillmore notes that Samson "represents the unlimited strength potential in man, which must be disciplined and dedicated to the service of Spirit."

Real-world Examples

Samson's story is relatable for anyone who has ever felt their talents or strengths were misused or led them astray, only to find redemption in a deeper understanding of their purpose.

Practical Applications

Awareness exercises can help you identify your unique strengths or 'Samson-like' attributes. Mindful decision-making can aid in utilizing these gifts responsibly.

Reader Reflections

1. What are your unique strengths, and how have they both empowered and challenged you?
2. Can you identify a moment where you felt 'betrayed' by misusing your talents or strengths?

Concluding Thoughts

The story of Samson serves as a metaphysical mirror for our own lives, urging us to handle our innate powers with wisdom and responsibility. It's a tale that captures the complexities of human strength, temptation, and the redeeming power of self-awareness.

Glossary of Metaphysical Interpretations for This Chapter

- Samson: Untamed spiritual strength within us
- Delilah: Temptation that leads to misuse of power
- Nazirite Vow: Symbolizes a sacred agreement or commitment to spiritual growth

- Philistine Temple: Represents structures or systems based on materialistic or lower consciousness

Additional Exercises

1. A guided meditation focusing on identifying and responsibly channeling your innate strengths.
2. Journaling prompts you to explore moments of strength, vulnerability, and redemption in your own life.

Chapter Twelve
In the Presence of Strength
and Rebellion - Samson's Story

A sizzling sound emanated from the grill outside, where hamburgers were transforming under the deft hand of Michael. Inside the kitchen, Ellery and Tillie were setting the table, their laughter and chatter a melody in the warm Sunday evening air. Their father's friend, Travis, an artist and musician, sat quietly on a barstool, eyes somewhat distant yet attentively observing the familial scene unfolding around him. A soul who never quite meshed with the societal mold, Travis was a mosaic of creativity and rebellion, yet enshrouded in a mist of unrealized potential and self-destruction through his battle with alcohol.

Once the grilled delights were brought inside and laid out enticingly on the table, everyone gathered around, with a noticeable shift in energy as they joined hands in a moment of gratitude before diving into their meal.

Amidst the hearty bites and casual conversation, Michael, ever the storyteller and philosophical guide, decided to steer the dialogue into the realms of another Biblical parable - the tale of Samson, a man of unparalleled strength yet besieged by his own vulnerabilities.

"Strength and weakness," began Michael, pausing to fill his cup, "are two facets of the same coin, inseparably intertwined within our human experience. The saga of Samson from the Book of Judges in the Old Testament demonstrates this dichotomy starkly."

Nailed It

As Michael unfolded Samson's story – a man blessed with superhuman strength, yet ultimately betrayed by his love, Delilah, and his own inability to master his desires – Travis, whose gaze had been languidly traversing his burger, lifted his eyes, an ember of curiosity flickering therein.

Ellery, familiar with Travis's own rebellious nature, gently nudged him into the dialogue. "Travis, doesn't Samson's anti-establishment stance resonate with you? His strength was a rebellion of sorts against the Philistines, yet, in the end, his internal vulnerabilities became his undoing."

Travis, finding a voice that was unexpectedly solid, responded, "Samson, from my perspective, is every person who has ever felt a dichotomy within them. A longing to defy oppressive forces, external or internal, yet chained by their own insecurities and cravings. His hair, the source of his strength, was also his Achilles' heel when it became known."

He paused, took a swig from his bottle, and continued, "We all have our 'hair,' our secret source of strength, but also a potential weak link if wielded imprudently."

Tillie, gentle yet assertive, probed further, "But doesn't his story also symbolize redemption? Despite his errors and betrayals, Samson's end was an act that delivered his people from oppression."

Michael, seizing the metaphysical thread, shared, "In

Charles Fillmore's metaphysical lens, Samson's strength symbolizes the innate spiritual power within each of us. His mistakes and eventual downfall mirror our struggles when we misapply our inherent spiritual faculties, letting them be guided by our lower nature, our 'Delilah.' His final act, where strength is regained, can be seen as a reawakening, where one transcends the lower self, allowing spiritual strength to guide actions."

In a brilliant contribution, Travis, pulling from the depths of his philosophical reservoir, shared a quote by Aldous Huxley: "Experience is not what happens to a man; it is what a man does with what happens to him."

The room seemed to pause, holding its breath as the words settled among them.

Travis, looking directly at Michael, elaborated, "We all have our battles, our strengths, and our Delilahs. It's what we do with them, how we navigate them, that defines our journey. Samson might have faltered, given his weaknesses, but don't we all? It's the act of standing up again, using our strengths for something beyond ourselves, that carves out redemption."

The table fell into a contemplative silence, each individual navigating through their internal landscape, contemplating their strengths, their vulnerabilities, and the interplay between the two.

As they eventually continued their meal, the atmosphere was

imbued with a new depth, a silent acknowledgment that each one of them, in their unique way, was traversing a journey peppered with strengths and weaknesses, triumphs and downfalls. Yet, in that shared moment, they were united, not just by the stories of ancient parables but by the contemporary, lived experiences that intertwined their paths in the sacred dance of life.

In that sacred space, amidst the mingling scents of grilled burgers and the dying embers of the day, they found a silent understanding that strength and vulnerability, rebellion and compliance, were simply different notes in the same melody that each soul was composing through the symphony of their life.

The narrative was not just in the ancient tales but was being written, rewritten, and lived in their every breath, every challenge, and every moment of reawakening.

A Prayer

Dear God,

I come before you today with gratitude for the strengths you have endowed me with, mindful of the responsibility that comes with these gifts. Like Samson, I am aware of the potential for my powers to be both a blessing and a curse.

Help me to wield my talents wisely to resist the temptations that can lead to their misuse. Let me find the balance that transforms raw potential into a force for good, serving both my own needs and those of others.

Inspire me with the wisdom to recognize when I stray from this path and grant me the humility to seek redemption and transformation. May my strengths, disciplined and aligned with your divine will, become instruments of positive change in this world.

In faith and humility, I pray.

Amen.

Journaling Prompts

1. Samson's downfall came through his relationship with Delilah. Have you ever felt that a relationship led you to misuse your talents or strengths? What lessons did you take from this experience?

2. The Nazirite vow symbolizes a sacred agreement or commitment to spiritual growth. What vows or commitments have you made in your personal or spiritual life, and how have they guided your actions?

3. Charles Fillmore interprets Samson as the untamed spiritual strength within each of us. Explore instances where you've felt this kind of raw, undirected power. How did you channel it constructively, or how could you do so in the future?

Chapter Thirteen
Ruth and Naomi

Introduction

The story of Ruth and Naomi is a touching tale of loyalty, love, and redemption. When viewed metaphysically, it serves as an allegory for the transformative power of commitment and devotion in our personal and spiritual lives.

Traditional Narrative

After the death of her husband and sons, Naomi decides to return to her homeland. Her daughter-in-law, Ruth, chooses to accompany her despite Naomi's attempts to dissuade her. Ruth's loyalty is rewarded when she marries Boaz, a relative of Naomi, thereby securing both their futures.

Biblical Context

This narrative is one of the few instances in the Bible that centers on the strength and agency of women. It highlights the virtues of loyalty, love and the importance of family ties.

Interfaith and Cultural Perspectives

The story of Ruth and Naomi has been embraced by both Jewish and Christian traditions and is often cited in discussions about the importance of strong family bonds and the virtues of kindness and loyalty.

Metaphysical Interpretation

According to Charles Fillmore's Metaphysical Bible Dictionary, Ruth symbolizes the soul's devotion to the Spirit, represented by Naomi. Their journey together indicates the soul's pilgrimage towards divine wisdom and understanding.

Quotes and References

Fillmore states, "Ruth, clinging to Naomi, portrays the soul that seeks the higher wisdom and is led by it into a new and more spiritual estate."

Real-world Examples

Many people can identify with the experience of choosing a difficult but rewarding path out of love and loyalty, whether it's in relationships, careers, or personal pursuits.

Practical Applications

Self-reflection exercises can help you identify the 'Naomi' in your life—the guiding wisdom that you feel devoted to—and the steps you can take to honor that devotion.

Reader Reflections

1. Have you ever made a difficult but rewarding choice out of loyalty or love?
2. What or who serves as your 'Naomi,' guiding you towards higher wisdom?

Concluding Thoughts

The story of Ruth and Naomi is not just a tale of loyalty and love but a metaphysical guide for those seeking to align their soul with divine wisdom. It exemplifies the transformative power of devotion and commitment in our spiritual journey.

Glossary of Metaphysical Interpretations for This Chapter

- Ruth: Soul's devotion to Spirit
- Naomi: Divine wisdom or higher self
- Boaz: Symbolizes the rewards or blessings that come from aligning with higher wisdom.

- Homeland: Represents a state of spiritual fulfillment or enlightenment

Additional Exercises

1. A guided meditation focused on recognizing and embracing your guiding wisdom or 'Naomi.'
2. Journaling prompts you to explore your experiences with loyalty, love, and the transformative power of devotion.

Chapter Thirteen

Loyalty Beyond Boundaries - The Tale of Ruth and Naomi

Spring had breathed a gentle vibrancy into the pasture that stretched luxuriously before Michael, Travis, Ellery, and Tillie. The caress of the breeze seemed to whisper ancient tales through the barbed wire fence, where two mellow draft mules and three majestic paint horses grazed languidly under the benevolent gaze of the afternoon sun. The golf balls soared through the air, their arcs storytelling in themselves before they landed, embedding their transient mark upon the landscape.

Travis's laugh, a harmonious blend of rebellion and innocence, wove through the air as he swung his driving wedge, his eyes gleaming with an unspoken tale of freedom and aimlessness. Michael, a contemplative expression molding his features, turned towards his daughters, witnessing the kaleidoscope of emotions dancing through their eyes as they engaged in this simple yet infinitely profound act of connection and togetherness.

Ellery, her swing steady and thoughtful, turned to her father, "What's our story today, Dad?"

Michael, lifting his gaze towards the azure expanse above, began, "Today, we delve into the story of Ruth and Naomi, a tale that speaks of unwavering loyalty, undying love, and the strength that emerges from the roots of steadfast solidarity."

As the narrative unfolded, weaving through the epochs to lay before them the journey of Ruth, a woman whose allegiance to her mother-in-law Naomi transcended the realms of obligation and ventured into the sacred territory of genuine, selfless love, a reflective hush enveloped the group.

"Ruth, despite her own path of potential comfort in her homeland, chose to tread the path of uncertainty and challenge, accompanying Naomi back to Bethlehem after they were both widowed," continued Michael, his voice a gentle, rhythmic cadence amidst the sound of golf balls being struck.

Tillie, a frown of contemplation etching her brow, interjected, "But why would she choose a path of potential strife over the comfort and familiarity of her own homeland?"

Michael, acknowledging the depth of the question with a nod, shared, "It's a testament to the power of authentic love and loyalty, Tillie. Ruth saw the pain and despair in Naomi and chose empathy and support over her own comfort. Her famous words, 'Where you go, I will go; where you lodge, I will lodge; your people shall be my people, and your God my God,' signify an unwavering commitment that is not bound by blood but by a conscious choice of unity and support."

Travis, silently absorbing the story, his eyes reflecting a storm of thoughts and memories, spoke, "Sometimes, choosing the path of loyalty, especially when it's not obligated, speaks volumes about the strength of relationships and the depth of human connection. It's an expression of love in its purest form, without expectations, without conditions."

As Helen Keller once profoundly said, "The best and most beautiful things in the world cannot be seen or even touched - they must be felt with the heart."

In a field where golf balls continued to slice through the air, each trajectory telling its own tale of force, direction, and intention, the story of Ruth and Naomi lingered, intertwining with their own narratives, prompting reflections on loyalty, love, and the paths chosen in the journey of life.

Michael, gazing at his daughters and then at Travis, recognized that the tales of the past were not mere stories but reflections of their own journeys, their struggles, choices, and the underlying currents of loyalty and love that bound them together against all odds.

And so, under the vast, embracing sky, amidst the echoes of swings, laughter, and philosophical musings, Ruth and Naomi lived again, not just as characters in an ancient tale but as symbols of the timeless, boundless love and loyalty that gently, yet indomitably, pulse through the veins of our shared humanity.

A Prayer

Dear God (or your preferred name for the Divine),

I come before you with a heart full of gratitude for the relationships that have enriched my life. Like Ruth's steadfast loyalty to Naomi, I am thankful for the bonds that have shown me the transformative power of love and commitment.

Help me recognize the guiding wisdom, my 'Naomi,' in my life that steers me toward higher understanding and purpose. Inspire me to be a 'Ruth' to those who need me, to stand by them as they have stood by me.

May my relationships be a source of spiritual growth, leading me and those I love closer to divine wisdom. Grant me the courage to make challenging but rewarding choices in the name of loyalty and love, just as Ruth did.

In your name, I pray with love and devotion.

Amen.

Journaling Prompts

1. The story centers around the agency and resilience of women. Write about a woman who has been a significant influence in your life, exploring how her strengths have impacted you.

2. Charles Fillmore interprets Ruth as symbolizing the soul's devotion to the Spirit, embodied by Naomi. Who or what represents your 'Naomi'—the guiding wisdom or higher self that you feel a devotion to?

3. Can you identify a 'Ruth' in your life? How has their loyalty influenced your journey?

4. Reflect on a relationship that has significantly transformed you, noting the role of commitment and devotion in that transformation.

Chapter Fourteen
Samuel Anoints Saul

Introduction

The story of Samuel anointing Saul as the first king of Israel addresses the complexities of leadership, divine appointment, and the human quest for governance. Metaphysically, it explores the tension between individual will and divine guidance.

Traditional Narrative

In the absence of strong leadership, the Israelites demand a king. Samuel, a prophet, is guided by God to anoint Saul as Israel's first king. Despite his initially humble response, Saul's reign eventually becomes problematic due to his disobedience to God's commands.

Biblical Context

Saul's anointing signifies a major shift in Israelite society—from a tribal community to a monarchy. It also reveals the pitfalls of leadership when it's disconnected from divine guidance.

Interfaith and Cultural Perspectives

The concept of a divinely-appointed leader is not unique to the Judeo-Christian tradition. Many cultures and religions have stories and philosophies that address the divine right or responsibility of rulers.

Metaphysical Interpretation

According to Charles Fillmore's Metaphysical Bible Dictionary, Samuel symbolizes the inner voice of divine guidance, while Saul represents the human ego or personal will that seeks external power.

Quotes and References

Fillmore notes that "Saul, the personal will, although anointed by spiritual understanding (Samuel), fails when it sets up its own kingdom independent of Divine Mind."

Real-world Examples

In organizational settings or even personal life, there can be a tendency to place disproportionate emphasis on external power or authority, often to the detriment of moral or spiritual considerations.

Practical Applications

Mindfulness practices can be used to cultivate a stronger connection with your inner 'Samuel,' allowing you to make decisions that are in alignment with a higher form of governance—your own divine guidance.

Reader Reflections

1. Have you ever found yourself in a leadership position where you felt disconnected from your inner guidance?
2. How do you reconcile your personal ambitions with your spiritual or ethical principles?

Concluding Thoughts

The story of Samuel anointing Saul serves as a cautionary tale about the risks of disconnecting leadership from divine or ethical guidance. It offers a metaphysical perspective on how to balance personal will with higher wisdom.

Glossary of Metaphysical Interpretations for This Chapter

- Samuel: Inner voice of divine guidance
- Saul: Human ego or personal will

- Anointing: Symbolic act of empowering or validating spiritual authority
- Israelites: Collective consciousness or community bound by spiritual principles

Additional Exercises

1. A guided meditation on tuning into your inner 'Samuel' to seek guidance in life decisions.
2. Journaling prompts that focus on instances where you had to balance your ambitions with your moral or ethical convictions.

Chapter Fourteen

Seeking the Anointed - Samuel and Saul

Early spring whispered its tender arrival through the budding trees that bordered the small park on the Square. Michael, Ellery, and Tillie found a gentle reprieve in its embrace as they settled into the swings, the subtle creak of the chains mingling with the soft rustlings of nature awakening from its wintry slumber.

The simplicity of the moment, swinging back and forth, allowed a serenity to weave through their beings, opening a space for stories and reflections to flow with ease. The town, with its quaintness and familiarity, cradled them in a comforting nostalgia, a backdrop that seemed apt for the unraveling of tales from ancient times.

Tillie, her eyes reflecting the delicate hues of the awakening flora, turned towards Michael, "What's our story today, Dad?"

With a gentle smile, Michael began, "Today, we dive into the tale of Samuel and Saul, exploring themes of leadership, divine guidance, and the intertwining of fate and free will   through the lens of Charles Fillmore's metaphysical insights."

As the story unfolded, describing Samuel, the prophet, being guided by the divine to anoint Saul as the first king of Israel despite the apparent incongruity of divine monarchy and human kingship, a thought-provoking quietude enveloped them.

"Charles Fillmore interprets the anointing of Saul not merely as a historical or divine event but as a metaphorical journey within," Michael continued, his voice a gentle cascade amidst the serene ambiance of the park. "Samuel symbolizes the inner guide or divine wisdom within us, while Saul represents the personal ego and willpower. The anointing signifies the acknowledgment and empowerment of our personal will by our inner divine wisdom."

Ellery, a spark of contemplation lighting her eyes, shared, "It's a potent symbolism, isn't it? Our inner wisdom, or 'Samuel,' anointing and recognizing the need for our personal will, our 'Saul,' to lead, yet always under the guidance of that deeper knowing."

The swings creaked gently as the trio pondered upon this interplay between the divine and the personal within, contemplating their own 'Sauls' and 'Samuels' and the dialogue between them.

Tillie, her voice thoughtful and soft, mused, "But what happens when our personal will, our 'Saul,' becomes too self-absorbed or loses its way? How does our inner 'Samuel' guide it back to a path of divine alignment?"

Michael, his eyes reflecting the depth of the query, responded, "Ah, that's where the ensuing chapters of Saul's reign speak to us, don't they? His journey unfolds as a cautionary tale of what occurs when the personal will disconnects from its divine guidance, spiraling into a path that eventually leads to its own undoing."

In the gentle sway of the swings and the soft murmur of the spring breeze, the words of philosopher Aristotle seemed to linger, "Dignity does not consist in possessing honors, but in deserving them."

And so, the story invites us to reflect upon our own

leadership, our own wielding of personal will," Michael continued, "urging us to remain attuned to our inner 'Samuel,' allowing it to guide and inform our 'Saul,' ensuring that our actions and choices emanate from a place of aligned divine wisdom."

In the simple act of swinging in that small park amidst the burgeoning spring, Michael, Ellery, and Tillie found themselves adrift in contemplations of leadership, will, and divine wisdom, recognizing that within the tales of the past lay the seeds of wisdom for the present and the future.

A Prayer

Dear God

As I navigate the challenges and opportunities of life, I seek Your guidance to balance my personal ambitions with divine wisdom. Just as Samuel anointed Saul, may my actions be anointed by Your higher guidance.

I recognize the tension between my inner Samuel and inner Saul—the pull between spiritual insight and earthly desires. Grant me the discernment to know when to listen to each and the wisdom to harmonize them in my decisions.

Help me become a leader who embodies not just authority but also compassion, integrity, and alignment with Your will. May my life be a reflection of the divine governance that Samuel symbolizes, ever cautious of the pitfalls that come with straying from Your path.

In Your name, I pray.

Amen.

Journaling Prompts

1. The story of Samuel and Saul serves as a cautionary tale about the pitfalls of leadership that veers away from ethical or divine guidance. Have you ever found yourself in a leadership position that tested your ethical boundaries? How did you navigate it?

2. Samuel symbolizes the inner voice of divine guidance, according to Charles Fillmore. Describe a time when you listened to your "inner Samuel" and made a decision based on intuition or higher wisdom.

3. Saul represents the human ego or personal will. Have there been times when your personal ambitions overshadowed your ethical or spiritual principles? What were the consequences?

4. Do you identify more with Samuel's divine guidance or Saul's human ego in your life? How can you bring more balance between the two?

Chapter Fifteen
David and Goliath

Introduction

The story of David and Goliath is perhaps one of the most iconic tales in the Bible, representing the triumph of the underdog. Metaphysically, it serves as a powerful example of how faith and inner strength can overcome seemingly insurmountable obstacles.

Traditional Narrative

Young David, armed only with a sling and stones, defeats Goliath, a towering Philistine warrior. This victory for the Israelites illustrates the power of faith and divine intervention.

Biblical Context

David's story is a turning point in Israelite history, marking the rise of a shepherd boy to the eventual king of Israel. It emphasizes the importance of faith in divine will over human might.

Interfaith and Cultural Perspectives

The David and Goliath narrative has permeated beyond religious contexts and into popular culture, symbolizing the classic struggle between the weak and the powerful.

Metaphysical Interpretation

According to Charles Fillmore's Metaphysical Bible Dictionary, David represents the spiritual consciousness that triumphs through alignment with divine principles, while Goliath symbolizes the intimidating obstacles or challenges that loom large in our human experience.

Quotes and References

Fillmore states, "David, as spiritual consciousness, uses 'smooth stones' or well-defined spiritual affirmations to defeat the fearsome Goliath of material consciousness."

Real-world Examples

We all face 'Goliaths' in our lives, be it in the form of challenges, fears, or doubts. Yet, like David, we often find that these giants are not invincible and can be overcome through inner resolve and faith.

Practical Applications

Visualization exercises can help you mentally prepare for challenges, just as David did. Affirmations can serve as your 'smooth stones,' equipping you with the confidence to face your obstacles.

Reader Reflections

1. What are the 'Goliaths' in your life, and how have you approached them?
2. Can you identify moments when your inner 'David' came to the forefront?

Concluding Thoughts

The story of David and Goliath isn't merely an epic tale of victory against the odds; it's a metaphysical guide to conquering the challenges that confront us. Through faith and inner strength, we, too, can overcome our 'Goliaths.'

Glossary of Metaphysical Interpretations for This Chapter

- David: Spiritual consciousness aligned with divine principles

- Goliath: Obstacles or challenges in human experience
- Sling and Stones: Tools or affirmations for spiritual empowerment
- Philistines: Representations of materialistic or lower consciousness

Additional Exercises

1. A guided meditation to identify and face your personal 'Goliaths.'
2. Journaling prompts exploring your victories and what they have taught you about your inner strength and resilience.

Chapter Fifteen

Reflections of Giants and Shepherds

In the embrace of spring, under a celestial sky, Michael, Tillie, Travis, and Travis's son Gabe encamped at a secluded cove by the lake. Their silhouettes, along with Gabe's quiet figure, cast by the flickering campfire, danced against the backdrop of the quiet wilderness.

As Travis adjusted his hammock and Michael secured the tent, Tillie and Gabe gathered around the campfire. Gabe, though reserved, watched with an intuitive gaze that missed little. The crackling fire orchestrated a melody for stories and reflections.

"You know, Dad," Tillie began, "Your stories have a way of igniting thoughts like this fire."

Nailed It

A soft chuckle emanated from Travis, his demeanor relaxed, and his gaze fixated on the cascading sparks ascending into the nocturnal abyss. "Perhaps, Tillie, stories are the fire of our minds, illuminating dark recesses and revealing paths otherwise unseen.

"Gabe nodded silently, his eyes reflecting deep thought.

Michael Started, "Today, let's explore one such path through the tale of David and Goliath, examining it through the lens of Charles Fillmore's metaphysical interpretations."

As the tale of the shepherd boy who slew a giant unfolded, Michael spoke of David representing love and courage and Goliath symbolizing our personal fears and obstacles that stand towering, seemingly insurmountable. David's victory illuminated the potency of inner spiritual strength, triumphing over formidable adversities.

"Fillmore would suggest," Michael continued, "that David, our embodiment of love and courage, doesn't shy away from Goliath, our internal fears and challenges. Instead, with faith in the divine and trust in his capabilities, he confronts and ultimately vanquishes his giant."

Tillie, contemplative, whispered, "Confronting our fears, our personal Goliaths, it's like peering into an abyss, isn't it? Knowing we must step forward, yet the vastness of what lies ahead can be paralyzing.

Travis, his voice softened yet solid, spoke, "Perhaps therein lies the essence, Tillie. To confront and engage with our Goliaths is to acknowledge and traverse our abyss. And remember what our friend Thoreau once said,"

With a deliberate pause, he recited, "'The mass of men lead lives of quiet desperation. What is called resignation is confirmed desperation.'"

The quote lingered amidst the embers, interweaving with the serenity of the lake and the profoundness of the celestial above.

Michael, absorbing the weight of the words, continued, "Thoreau here might be suggesting that many of us, in confronting our Goliaths, choose resignation, quietly succumbing to our fears and challenges instead of confronting them. It's a silent desperation, an acceptance of the abyss without exploration or attempt to traverse it.

Gabe, usually quiet, interjected insightfully, "Maybe it's about finding courage within to face that abyss."

As the night deepened, their reflections intertwined with the wilderness around them. Gabe, understood the depth of their conversation, his quick insights adding a unique dimension to their contemplations.

Together, they found understanding in the metaphor of giants and shepherds – confronting each Goliath brings one closer to transcending the silent desperations within.

Beyond Doubt

Act 1: The Victory of Imagination.

Inside the complex vastness of a person's mind, a constant battle was underway. Arrayed in battle formation were the Israelites—flashes of optimism, glimmers of creativity, and fragments of noble aspirations. Each one was like a star on the horizon of possibility, illuminating paths to unexplored dreams and untapped potentials.

Opposite them, shrouded in a dark mist of uncertainty, were the Philistines—imposing barriers of fear, towering walls of doubt, and swirling vortexes of insecurity. They were the obstacles that whispered, "You can't" or "You're not good enough," feeding off any attempt to push beyond the comfort zone.

Among this legion of darkness stood Goliath, the epitome of inner turmoil. He was more than just a thought; he was a towering giant made of impenetrable armor of pessimism and a sword of fatalism. With each step he took, the earth of the mental landscape quaked. Every day, like clockwork, he would step forward and bellow across the field of consciousness, issuing his challenge.

"Who dares to defeat me? Who thinks they can overcome the power of doubt and fear?" His voice echoed, reverberating through the neurons and synapses, shaking the very core of the Israelites' hopes.

The Israelites, always teetering on the brink of courage,

would quiver at his taunts. They longed to break free to advance toward the new territories of love, achievement, and self-worth. But each time they mustered the courage to make a move, the image of Goliath stomping forth was enough to make them retreat. Their spears of intent drooped; their shields of resilience wavered.

And so, day after day, the stalemate persisted. The Israelites—those fragments of positive thoughts and desires—remained encamped, their dreams suspended in a purgatory of inaction, waiting for something or someone to tip the balance.

It was a battlefield with no victors, only casualties—casualties of unfulfilled potential, untaken risks, and unrealized dreams. But change, as it always does, was on the horizon. And its name was David.

Act 2: The Arrival of Imagination (David)

One day, a new presence entered this fraught landscape of the mind, like a fresh breeze cutting through stagnant air. David—the shepherd of imagination—strolled in, free from the heavy armor of past failures or the burdensome weapons of overthinking. His mere presence felt like a sunbeam breaking through a cloudy sky, promising the warmth of renewed possibilities.

David wasn't a warrior by traditional standards. He carried no sword, no shield, no artillery of skepticism or cynicism. Instead, he had a simple sling, an unassuming yet powerful tool. This sling represented the ability to visualize—to take intangible thoughts and mold them into shapes and scenarios that could influence reality.

And from the riverbed of consciousness, David selected five smooth stones. Each one was an affirmation, a crystallized belief formed from the waters of positivity. "I am capable," "I am worthy," "I am loved," "I will succeed," "I choose happiness." These were the stones he chose, each one as round and firm as the convictions they stood for.

As he moved toward the field of battle, the Israelites sensed his presence, and a murmur spread among them. It was as if someone had tuned a guitar string, bringing it into perfect harmony; they felt uplifted and rejuvenated. Their spears of intent no longer drooped; their shields of resilience steadied. It was as if hope had arrived, personified.

David, with his sling slung over his shoulder and his pocket full of affirmations, positioned himself at the front of the Israelite formation. His eyes met Goliath's—a moment that transcended the mere locking of gazes. It was the collision of two worlds, two ideologies, two entirely different understandings of what was possible and what was not.

For the first time, Goliath felt a twinge of uncertainty, though he masked it well behind a scornful laugh. But David knew better; he sensed it the way a shepherd senses a storm approaching.

"Goliath," David spoke softly yet firmly, "your reign of doubt ends today."

The giant roared with laughter, a sound that reverberated like thunder across the landscape of the mind. But David stood his ground, sling at the ready. For the first time, the Israelites didn't retreat in fear; instead, they watched with bated breath, poised for what was to come.

Act 3: The Confrontation

David stood at the frontline, a humble figure against the looming presence of Goliath. The air was thick with anticipation, like the pause between the conductor's baton lift and the orchestra's first note. The Israelites held their collective breath, their spears of intent and shields of resilience tingling with a newfound sense of potential.

Goliath laughed, the sound echoing through the canyons and valleys of the mind. "You challenge me with pebbles and a sling? You think your pathetic tools can bring me down?"

His words were saturated with mockery, emblematic of the self-doubt and ridicule that often infest our thoughts when we dare to aim higher, to transform our lives.

David met Goliath's gaze, unwavering. "It's not the tools that matter, but the hands that wield them."

For the first time, Goliath felt a tremor of uncertainty course through him. This was new. This was different. This confrontation didn't fit the script that had been played out day after day on this mental battlefield. David, undeterred by the giant's size or his piercing words, ignited a flicker of doubt within the very entity built of it.

David tightened his grip on the sling, its leather straps

imbued with the essence of visualization—each twist and knot representing the countless shapes and scenarios one could conjure through the power of imagination.

"As long as I stand here," David continued, "I stand with the conviction that I am more than my doubts, more than my fears, and certainly more than you, Goliath."

Goliath sneered, trying to maintain his façade of invincibility. "Fine words for a shepherd. Let's see if you can back them up."

David nodded, an understated but definitive affirmation of his readiness. "I don't think—I know."

The mental landscape seemed to hold its breath as if every thought, every fragment of emotion, waited for what would come next. Would David's sling and stones be enough to break the cycle of stagnation? Could imagination truly conquer fear?

With the tension at its zenith, David reached into his pouch and pulled out a stone—an affirmation carefully chosen for this pivotal moment.

Act 4: The Sling and the Stone

David held the stone between his fingers, feeling its smooth surface. It was a simple rock, but inscribed within it was the affirmation: "I am capable." This was the stone that he had chosen, the belief that he now fully embraced.

He carefully placed the stone into the pouch of his sling, positioning it just so. With a deep breath, he began to swing the sling above his head, each rotation amplifying the power of the stone's affirmation. As the sling spun, David visualized his deepest fears disintegrating into stardust, replaced by a radiant pillar of self-assurance and capability.

Then, with a climactic release that seemed to ripple through the very fabric of the mental world, he let the stone fly.

The stone soared through the air, a speeding bullet of concentrated belief. Time seemed to slow as it closed the distance between David and Goliath as if every thought and emotion were holding its breath, suspended in anticipation.

And then it struck—right between Goliath's eyes, at the very center of his forehead, the seat of his thought and the nexus of his belief system.

For a fraction of a second, the giant's eyes widened in disbelief, as if he had just been awakened from a long, enduring nightmare. Then, with a thunderous crash that shook the entire landscape, Goliath fell. His colossal body hit the ground, his armor of pessimism shattered, his sword of fatalism clattering away into oblivion.

The giant of doubt and fear was defeated, not by brute force, but by a single, undeniable belief hurled from the sling of imagination.

David stood there, the sling now hanging loosely by his side, his face glowing with the serene light of victory. The stone had found its mark and, in doing so, had changed the rules of engagement on this battlefield of the mind.

Act 5: Triumph and Transformation

In the wake of Goliath's fall, a ripple of disbelief spread through the ranks of the Philistines. The dark clouds of fear, doubt, and insecurity began to disperse as if a strong wind had scattered them. What had once seemed like an impenetrable wall of negativity was now broken, and the Philistines found themselves leaderless, their cornerstone of fear toppled.

Sensing the seismic shift in the landscape, the Israelites roared to life. Their spears of intent were no longer drooping; their shields of resilience now shone brilliantly. They surged forward, reclaiming lost territories in the realms of creativity, love, ambition, and self-worth. No longer did they hesitate at the boundaries of their dreams; they broke through, each thought a warrior, each aspiration a hero.

David watched as the Israelites charged forward, his heart swelling with pride and gratitude. He had done it; he had shown them, and himself, that the seemingly insurmountable could be conquered, that giants could be felled by the sheer force of belief and imagination.

And as the Israelites continued their advance, driving the remnants of the Philistines into the distant corners of the mind, David stood as a beacon—a living testament to the transformative power of imagination, visualization, and affirmation.

The mental battlefield had been altered forever. What was once a landscape dominated by fear and stagnation was now a flourishing garden of potential and opportunity. And at its center stood David, sling in hand, his pocket empty of stones but his heart full of endless possibilities.

A Prayer

Dear Divine Source,

Guide us as we navigate the battlefields of our minds, strewn with fears and uncertainties. Bestow upon us the wisdom to recognize our inner 'David,' armed with the sling of imagination and the stones of affirmation. Lead us towards a life that manifests our fullest potential, a life where our Goliaths are but stepping stones on our path to spiritual enlightenment. As we strive to align our actions and thoughts with Your divine principles, may we continue to find strength and courage, just as David did on that fateful day.

Amen.

Journaling Prompts

1. Stone of Affirmation: Identify one affirmation that could be your "smooth stone" to face your personal Goliath. How does this affirmation resonate with you, and why do you think it can be powerful?

2. David's Qualities: What traits or qualities make your inner 'David' unique? Is it creativity, resilience, or perhaps a strong sense of justice?

3. The Battlefield of Your Mind: Reflect on a situation where you felt trapped by fear or doubt. How did that mental 'battlefield' look like for you, and how did you—or could you—overcome it?

4. Leaders of Doubt: Who or what are the 'Philistines' in your life that nourish your fears and insecurities? Are they external influences or perhaps internal thought patterns?

5. Tools in Hand: Like David's sling, what simple but effective tools do you possess that can help you conquer your challenges? These could be skills, habits, or mindsets.

Chapter Sixteen
David and Bathsheba

Introduction

The story of David and Bathsheba is a complex narrative of lust, betrayal, and the misuse of power. On a metaphysical level, it explores the consequences of being out of alignment with divine principles and offers insights into the process of repentance and redemption.

Traditional Narrative

King David becomes infatuated with Bathsheba, the wife of Uriah the Hittite, a loyal soldier. To have Bathsheba for himself, David arranges for Uriah to be killed in battle. He marries Bathsheba, but the act brings divine displeasure, and they suffer the loss of their child.

Biblical Context

This story marks a significant moral lapse in David's life and serves as a cautionary tale about the dangers of unchecked power and desire. It also introduces the theme of divine justice and redemption as David eventually repents.

Interfaith and Cultural Perspectives

The themes of betrayal, consequences, and repentance are universal, appearing in various cultural and religious stories. They serve as moral lessons, warning against the misuse of power.

Metaphysical Interpretation

In Charles Fillmore's Metaphysical Bible Dictionary, David represents spiritual consciousness, and this story illustrates what can happen when spiritual consciousness is overtaken by ego-driven desires, symbolized by Bathsheba.

Quotes and References

Fillmore says, "David's yielding to temptation shows how even the spiritual consciousness can be misled when it leans too much to the understanding of the personal man."

Real-world Examples

The narrative provides a timeless lesson on the consequences of letting personal desires overshadow ethical considerations, something many people can relate to in varying contexts, from personal relationships to professional settings.

Practical Applications

The story encourages self-examination, inviting us to consider the temptations that could potentially lead us astray and the steps we can take to realign ourselves with higher ethical and spiritual principles.

Reader Reflections

1. Have you ever faced a situation where your desires conflicted with your ethical or spiritual beliefs?
2. What actions did you take to realign yourself with your principles?

Concluding Thoughts

The tale of David and Bathsheba serves as both a warning and a guide. It illustrates the pitfalls of acting on ego-driven desires but also provides a roadmap for repentance and realignment with divine principles.

Glossary of Metaphysical Interpretations for This Chapter

- David: Spiritual consciousness
- Bathsheba: Ego-driven desires
- Uriah: Represents loyalty or virtues that are compromised
- Repentance: The mental and emotional process of returning to alignment with divine principles

Additional Exercises

1. A guided meditation focusing on identifying and letting go of ego-driven desires.
2. Journaling prompts to explore times you felt out of alignment and the actions you took for reconciliation.

Chapter Sixteen

Pondering Faithfulness Amidst Fragility

The evening unveiled itself subtly, a tender ballet of lingering daylight intertwining with the quiet arrival of night. On the back porch, Michael and Travis, enveloped in the modest comforts of familiarity and camaraderie, spoke candidly amidst the intimate ambiance created by the caress of a gentle spring breeze and the resonance of distant nocturnal melodies.

Glasses clinked softly, a muted symphony of beer bottles and whiskey glasses providing a melodic accompaniment to their shared vulnerabilities and reflections.

Michael, his gaze anchored to the horizon, where the final blush of the sunset whispered tales of the day gone by, began to weave a narrative into their musings. "Travis, what do you think of the story of David and Bathsheba?"

Travis, nodding, his eyes reflecting the delicate dance of nearby fireflies, responded, "The king who witnessed a beauty so entrancing, it led him down a path strewn with deceit and sin, right?"

"Exactly," Michael whispered, allowing the tale to unfold - David, a king, revered and exalted, yet succumbing to the frailty of his desires and orchestrating the demise of an innocent man, Uriah, to conceal his transgressions.

As Michael spoke, the air seemed to constrict slightly, an unseen weight delicately descending upon the porch, a soft acknowledgment of the humanity and flaw exhibited by the biblical king.

He pondered aloud, "David saw something he desired, something not his to take, and yet he reached out and took it regardless. Charles Fillmore would perhaps perceive David as our spiritual identity and Bathsheba as our human experiences and desires. Uriah, her rightful husband, might symbolize our lawful connection to experiences   through virtue and righteousness."

Travis, absorbing the layered narrative, mused, "Even a king, a man of formidable power and divine favor, faltered, choosing a path forged in deceit and self-serving actions."

The sound of a car pulling into the driveway punctured their contemplation, signaling Ellery's return. Her presence is a gentle reminder of the juxtaposition between familial ties and the isolation found in personal tribulations.

As she stepped onto the porch, Ellery, sensing the profundity of their conversation, inquired softly, "What tales are being spun here tonight?"

Michael, welcoming her with a smile, shared, "We've wandered down the path of David and Bathsheba, exploring the corridors of desires, betrayals, and the often blurred lines separating virtue from vice."

Ellery, her eyes mirroring a reservoir of wisdom and understanding beyond her years, contributed, "Our pursuits, particularly those conceived in moments of weakness and selfishness, can have rippling effects, cascading through the lives of others, much like a stone disrupting a once placid pond."

At this moment, the pond of their existence seemed to pause, awaiting the descent of another stone, another choice to disrupt its tranquility.

Travis, his words gently staggering under the influence of whiskey, confided, "I've pondered, many a time, whether my struggles, my choices to resist conformity, and to pursue my passions, albeit have cast stones into the pond of my own marriage. We've weathered storms, my wife and I, yet I wonder if the ripples from my stones have distorted her reflections over the years."

Michael, taking a drink, admitted, "We, like David, each navigate through our fields of choices, sowing seeds which will one day blossom into consequences, anticipated or otherwise. I, too, have wandered through three marriages and often questioned the reflections I've left in their respective ponds."

In a profound silence, the trio allowed the threads of contemplation to weave around them, recognizing the shared humanity in their individual journeys. Michael, Travis, and Ellery, amidst their quiet introspection under the soft embrace of the spring night, found a collective comfort, a unity amidst the tales of ancient kings and modern musings.

Here, on a modest back porch, they acknowledged the cascading ripples of their choices, contemplating the stories that had been and those yet to be written, gently bound by the acknowledgment that every choice, every cast stone, gently shapes the reflections witnessed in the ponds of their existence.

A Prayer

Divine Creator, we come before you humbled by the lessons of life and the ever-present challenges that test our moral and spiritual alignment. Grant us the wisdom to recognize our missteps, the courage to make amends, and the strength to adhere to higher principles that reflect Your divine essence. May we always be vigilant in our actions so that we may walk a path that is pleasing to You, filled with integrity, love, and spiritual enlightenment. Amen.

Journaling Prompts:

1. Reflect on a moment in your life when you felt a strong desire that contradicted your ethical or spiritual principles. How did you feel at that moment?

2. Write about a time you recognized you had misused your power, whether it was in a relationship, at work, or in a social setting. What steps did you take to make amends?

3. In what ways have you personally experienced the concept of "divine justice," either as a giver or a receiver?

4. Considering Charles Fillmore's metaphysical interpretations, have you identified any aspects of your spiritual consciousness that have been compromised by ego-driven desires? How so?

5. The story of David and Bathsheba ends with David's repentance and the hope for redemption. Have you ever felt a deep need to repent for something? Describe the experience and how it impacted your life moving forward.

Chapter Seventeen
Solomon's Wisdom

Introduction

Solomon, the son of David and Bathsheba, is celebrated for his unparalleled wisdom. In metaphysical terms, the story illustrates the power of divine understanding and discernment in governing our lives.

Traditional Narrative

Solomon becomes king after David and prays for wisdom above all else. God grants his request, and Solomon gains fame for his wise judgments, including the famous case of the two women claiming the same baby, which he resolves by suggesting dividing the child, thereby revealing the true mother.

Biblical Context

Solomon's reign is often seen as a high point in Israelite history, marked by prosperity and peace. His wisdom is considered his defining characteristic, although later in life, he strays from this path, succumbing to material and idolatrous temptations.

Interfaith and Cultural Perspectives

Wisdom as a divine attribute is highly valued across multiple faith traditions. Solomon himself is recognized in Islamic tradition as a prophet and wise king.

Metaphysical Interpretation

According to Charles Fillmore's Metaphysical Bible Dictionary, Solomon symbolizes the "peaceable, constructive domain of the mind," where wisdom reigns. The women in the famous judgment represent conflicting desires or claims that require discernment.

Quotes and References

Fillmore points out that Solomon's wisdom was not just intellectual but spiritual, "built on understanding and love, balanced by judgment and discernment."

Real-world Examples

In today's complex world, we are often faced with difficult decisions requiring a balance of intellect, emotion, and ethics. Solomon's wisdom serves as a model for such balanced decision-making.

Practical Applications

Practicing discernment can start with small, everyday choices. Mindfulness techniques can help you become more aware of your decision-making processes and their alignment with your principles.

Reader Reflections

1. Have you encountered situations that required Solomon-like wisdom?
2. How do you balance intellectual and ethical considerations when making decisions?

Concluding Thoughts

Solomon's wisdom serves as an inspiration for attaining a harmonious balance in our mental and spiritual faculties. Even as Solomon later strays from his wisdom, his story provides a cautionary note, reminding us to maintain our alignment with divine principles.

Glossary of Metaphysical Interpretations for This Chapter

- Solomon: Peaceable, constructive domain of the mind
- Wisdom: Divine understanding and discernment
- The two women: Conflicting desires or claims
- The baby: Unity or harmony at stake

Additional Exercises

1. A guided meditation focusing on tapping into your inner wisdom for discernment.

2. Journaling prompts that explore instances where you had to exercise wisdom and how those experiences shaped you.

Chapter Seventeen

The Harvest of Understanding

A symphony of vibrant colors filled the landscape as Michael and Travis stood by the modest pond, their fishing lines dancing gently with the caress of the wind. The boundless fields stretched out around them, while a quarter mile to the north, Michael's house stood silent, observant amidst the spring splendor.

The sun, benevolently casting its warm embrace upon the land, kissed their skins and mirrored in the tranquil water before them. Michael cast his line, the green jig disappearing beneath the surface, and mused aloud, "Travis, does the tale of King Solomon ring in your ears?"

Travis, eyes fixed on the serene water, nodded, "The man who, when offered anything, chooses wisdom over wealth or power."

As the words lingered, a crappie tugged gently at Michael's line. With a practiced hand, he reeled it in, the fish shimmering with vitality amidst its struggle.

As he unhooked the creature, releasing it back to the depths from whence it came, Michael articulated his thoughts, "Solomon, in his divine wisdom, understood that knowledge was the cornerstone upon which all other blessings were built. In his story, perhaps we might perceive wisdom as an acknowledgment of our interconnectedness and understanding as a recognition of the underlying unity of all life. Charles Fillmore might posit that Solomon's wisdom reflects our inherent ability to judge, discern, or comprehend rightly, deriving from a deep inner knowing, rather than learned knowledge."

Travis, absorbed in the metaphysical undertones, mused, "Solomon could dissect the complexities and paradoxes of human nature and existence, all while maintaining a perspective rooted in divine wisdom and understanding."

The two men, enveloped in a cocoon of nature's beauty and the tranquility of their shared companionship, found comfort in the philosophical explorations afforded by the ancient tale.

As they conversed, a playful rustling emerged from the nearby field, announcing the arrival of Michael's brother's dogs, their tails wagging, eyes gleaming with the simplicity and joy found in the present moment.

In their canine exuberance, a reflection shimmered, hinting at an unspoken wisdom rooted in being rather than pondering, doing rather than questioning. Travis, a gentle smile adorning his face, whispered, "Sometimes, I find, wisdom is exhibited most purely in beings that do not ponder their existence but merely exist, finding joy in the simplicity of being."

Michael, observing the dogs as they frolicked, conceded, "And therein lies a wisdom, perhaps akin to Solomon's – an understanding of the harmony that exists when we embrace the present, acknowledging the divine whole of which we are a part."

They continued to fish, the crappie generously offering themselves, only to be gratefully returned to their aquatic haven following a moment of acknowledgment and appreciation. The conversations wove through time, intertwining biblical wisdom, philosophical reflections, and the silent, profound understanding mirrored in the eyes of the frolicking dogs.

As the day meandered towards its conclusion, the sun gently descending behind Michael's distant home, the men found a peaceful accord, recognizing that wisdom, whether gleamed from ancient tales or reflected in the eyes of our four-legged companions, resides not in the answers we seek but in our ability to appreciate and navigate the infinite questions birthed in our seeking.

In the shared silence that followed, the whispering wind and the gentle rustling of spring leaves sang a lullaby of timeless wisdom and transient moments, forever etched into the firmament of their beings.

A Prayer

Divine Source of Wisdom, we seek your guidance in our daily lives as we navigate the complexities and challenges that come our way. Grant us the discernment to make choices that align with your divine principles and the courage to prioritize true wisdom over fleeting desires. May our minds and hearts be balanced sanctuaries of understanding, love, and good judgment, much like the peaceable domain Solomon once symbolized. Amen.

Journaling Prompts:

1. Reflect on a moment when you had to make a difficult decision, similar to Solomon's judgment. How did you approach it, and what guided your decision-making?

2. In what ways have you balanced intellectual reasoning with emotional understanding when faced with a dilemma? Was the outcome satisfying?

3. How do you personally define wisdom? Is it more intellectual, spiritual, or a combination of both? Give an example to illustrate your point.

4. Solomon was celebrated for his wisdom but later in life succumbed to material and idolatrous temptations. Can you relate to experiencing a high point in your ethical or spiritual life and then facing a lapse or challenge?

5. Wisdom is valued across various cultures and religions. Are there any figures or teachings from other traditions that have inspired your own understanding of wisdom? Describe them and their impact on you.

Chapter Eighteen
Elijah and the Prophets of Baal

Introduction

The dramatic face-off between Elijah and the prophets of Baal is a stirring testament to the power of faith and the fallacy of false idols. Metaphysically, it explores the tension between true spiritual insight and misguided worldly pursuits.

Traditional Narrative

Elijah, a prophet of God, challenges the prophets of Baal to prove whose deity is real. Despite their frantic efforts, the prophets of Baal are unable to summon fire to consume their offering. Elijah, with a simple prayer, summons divine fire, proving the supremacy of God.

Biblical Context

Set against the backdrop of a society that had turned to idol worship, this story is a decisive moment in Israelite history. It serves as a vivid reminder of the need for genuine spiritual connection over hollow ritualism.

Interfaith and Cultural Perspectives

The motif of a divine challenge to prove the validity of spiritual paths is common in various traditions, often emphasizing the distinction between true and false spiritual practices.

Metaphysical Interpretation

In Charles Fillmore's Metaphysical Bible Dictionary, Elijah symbolizes the spiritual perception that discerns the true from the false. Baal and his prophets represent materialism and false beliefs that divert us from spiritual truth.

Quotes and References

Fillmore suggests that Elijah's ability to call down divine fire indicates "the consuming power of true spiritual insight over false beliefs and materialism."

Real-world Examples

Many people face 'prophets of Baal' in the form of distractions, false promises, or superficial solutions that deviate from genuine personal and spiritual growth.

Practical Applications

A disciplined practice of mindfulness or meditation can help you hone your 'inner Elijah,' enabling you to discern what is genuinely valuable and what is a mere distraction in your life.

Reader Reflections

1. Have you faced situations where you had to distinguish between true and false paths?
2. How do you cultivate your 'inner Elijah' to make better decisions?

Concluding Thoughts

Elijah and the Prophets of Baal serve as a cautionary tale against succumbing to the allure of false beliefs or material pursuits. It teaches us the value of genuine spiritual insight in discerning the truth.

Glossary of Metaphysical Interpretations for This Chapter

- Elijah: Spiritual perception that discerns true from false
- Prophets of Baal: Materialism and false beliefs
- Divine fire: Consuming power of spiritual truth
- Offering: What we bring to our spiritual practice, either genuinely or falsely

Additional Exercises

1. A guided meditation focusing on discerning your true spiritual path.
2. Journaling prompts exploring how you distinguish between genuine and false beliefs or pursuits in your life.

Chapter Eighteen
In Quietude, A Fire Ignites

Michael eased the front door open, his frame shadowed by the lingering weariness of a grueling twelve-hour shift welding. The soft, warm glow of the kitchen lights beckoned, revealing the safe harbor of the home where Tillie and Ellery dwelled, each ensconced in their own worlds of creation and preparation. Tillie, her fingers dancing with colored pencils, birthed new worlds upon her sketchpad, while Ellery, amidst a palette of colors and tools, painted her visage with subtle, artful strokes.

As Michael settled into a worn, welcoming chair, a can of beer whispering open, he gazed towards his daughters, finding peace amidst the juxtaposition of their focused activities. Tillie's pencils sketched dreams into existence, while Ellery, in her blossoming into night's adventures, revealed both the vitality and transience of youth.

The whisper of a thought cascaded through Michael's consciousness, nudging towards a tale from an ancient tome, "Girls, amidst the tales told by prophets and kings, a story lives - of Elijah and the prophets of Baal."

Tillie's pencils paused mid-stroke while Ellery turned, her eyes reflecting the curiosity birthed in tales of old, "Prophets?"

With a soft nod, Michael began, "Elijah, a prophet, challenged the prophets of Baal, seeking to reveal the unwavering might of his God. They each built an altar, laying out a sacrifice, beseeching their deities to set ablaze the offerings without mortal ignition."

A subtle smile adorned his lips, "Elijah, with serene assurance, doused his altar in water, not once, but thrice. In profound faith, he called upon his God, and fire descended from the heavens, consuming the saturated offering, stones, and soil, leaving naught but divine assertion in its wake."

Ellery's fingers lingered amidst her cosmetics, "A tale of faith triumphing over doubt?"

Michael agreed, yet his voice carried a whisper of contemplation, "Indeed, E. Yet, perhaps, beneath the layers of divine demonstrations and religious tenets, lies a subtler, more personal unveiling. Charles Fillmore might guide us towards seeing Elijah's unwavering faith as a reflection of our own internal, undying flame of faith and inner knowing, eternally alive amidst the floods of doubt and external tumult."

Tillie, her eyes reflecting the gentle flames of inquisitiveness, questioned, "Does faith always ignite the fires?"

Michael, finding resonance in her query, shared a pearl from the depths of philosophical ponderings, "C.S. Lewis once stated that faith is the art of holding on to things your reason has once accepted, in spite of your changing moods.'"

As the words lingered amidst the trio, the whispering of pencils on paper and the subtle clicking of cosmetic cases offered a melodic accompaniment to their ponderings.

Ellery, her gaze both in the now and on unseen horizons, pondered, "Faith, then, is our own fire, illuminating our path even when drenched in the waters of uncertainty and challenge?"

In silent agreement, Michael raised his can, a subtle salute to the wisdoms birthed in ancient tales and the timeless journey of understanding, ever unwinding within and around them.

Tillie, Ellery, and Michael, bound by blood and the ever-dancing flames of questioning, seeking, and being, found a quietude amidst their shared evening, recognizing that within each of them, an indomitable flame of faith and inner wisdom eternally ablaze, eternally guiding, through generations, tales, and transient moments.

A Prayer

Eternal Source of Wisdom and Truth, we come before you, seeking the clarity and courage exemplified by Elijah. Help us to identify and turn away from our own "prophets of Baal," those material pursuits and shallow beliefs that divert us from your Divine presence. Empower us with your "divine fire," the consuming power of true spiritual insight, so that we may burn away falsehoods and illuminate our paths with Your eternal truth. Amen.

Journaling Prompts:

1. Describe a situation where you faced your own "prophets of Baal," those distractions or false beliefs that pulled you away from what you knew was right or true. How did you handle it?

2. What are the 'offerings' you bring to your own spiritual or personal growth? Are they genuine investments or mere ritualistic practices?

3. Consider a moment when you had an 'Elijah moment,' a flash of insight that helped you discern between a true and false path in your life. What led to this realization?

4. The story of Elijah and the Prophets of Baal is also a story of courage in standing against popular but false beliefs. Have you ever had to stand alone in your convictions? Describe the experience and the outcome.

5. Many spiritual traditions talk about the idea of discernment or recognizing the truth. Are there teachings from other religious or philosophical traditions that have influenced your understanding of discernment? What are they, and how have they shaped your beliefs?

Chapter Nineteen
Isaiah's Prophecies

Introduction

Isaiah's prophecies serve as beacons of hope and warning in the midst of political and spiritual upheaval. Metaphysically, they offer deep insights into the transformative power of faith and the enduring nature of divine principles.

Traditional Narrative

Isaiah, a prophet in the Kingdom of Judah, conveys messages from God that span both cautionary tales and hopeful visions. He foretells the fall of nations, the coming of a messiah, and a new, harmonious world order.

Biblical Context

Isaiah lived during a time of great turmoil, including the Assyrian invasion and the spiritual decline of Israel. His prophecies are complex, interweaving imminent political events with eschatological visions.

Interfaith and Cultural Perspectives

Isaiah's prophecies have had a profound impact across religious traditions, including Christianity and Islam, and have been interpreted in various ways, highlighting the universal quest for divine justice and a better future.

Metaphysical Interpretation

According to Charles Fillmore's Metaphysical Bible Dictionary, Isaiah represents the illuminative, predictive aspect of our own consciousness that foresightedly perceives the outcomes of staying aligned or misaligned with spiritual principles.

Quotes and References

Fillmore states, "Isaiah's prophecies symbolize the spiritual insights that guide us toward fulfilling our divine potential while also warning us of the pitfalls of straying from divine law."

Real-world Examples

Just as Isaiah foresaw both doom and redemption based on collective choices, individuals today experience consequences and opportunities based on their alignment with spiritual or ethical principles.

Practical Applications

To activate your 'inner Isaiah,' develop a practice of introspection and contemplation to better understand the spiritual laws that govern your life and to make informed choices accordingly.

Reader Reflections

1. Have you ever felt like you had a prophetic insight or foresight into a situation?
2. How do you apply spiritual or ethical principles in making future decisions?

Concluding Thoughts

Isaiah's prophecies stand as timeless reminders of the potential consequences and rewards that come with our choices. They invite us to be vigilant in aligning ourselves with spiritual principles for a more harmonious future.

Glossary of Metaphysical Interpretations for This Chapter

- Isaiah: Illuminative, predictive consciousness
- Prophecies: Spiritual insights that guide and warn

- Fall of nations: Consequences of collective spiritual misalignment
- Coming of a messiah: Hope for redemption and enlightenment

Additional Exercises

1. A guided meditation focusing on cultivating foresight and spiritual discernment.
2. Journaling prompts to explore your intuitive insights and how they have guided or warned you in the past.

Chapter Nineteen

Seeds in the Wind, Echoes in the Soul

A gentle, warm breeze caressed the vast, open fields of the countryside, whispering tales of distant lands as it rustled through the tall grasses lining the gravel driveway. Michael and Tillie, enshrouded in the tranquil embrace of a bright summer day, strolled toward the mailbox, their steps accompanied by the symphony of nature and the soft crunch of gravel beneath their feet.

Michael, his gaze journeying across the vibrant, emerald pasture, where horses, embodiments of boundless freedom and tranquil strength, grazed amidst wildflowers, contemplated the synchronicities life subtly unveils.

"Tillie," Michael's voice, a soft melody amidst the whispers of the wind, "have you ever pondered upon the seeds carried upon these summer breezes, journeying towards unforeseen destinies, destined to birth life wherever they descend?"

Tillie, her eyes reflecting the boundless skies, responded, "Dad, it's like they carry hidden promises, isn't it? Tales yet to be unveiled, blossoming wherever they find solace."

A gentle nod from Michael affirmed her ponderings. "Tillie, your thoughts bring to heart the prophecies of Isaiah from the ancient texts. A prophet, Isaiah, spoke of what was to come, of hopes, sufferings, and renewals, much like the seeds, carrying within them tales of potential, promising life amidst desolation."

As they approached the mailbox, its form a silent sentinel amidst the vast openness, he continued, "He spoke of a shoot coming up from a stump, a new branch out of roots, symbolizing renewal amidst destruction, and hope persisting amidst despair."

Tillie, her fingers dancing amidst the wildflowers lining their path, softly queried, "Are we, too, bearers of prophecies, Dad, in the seeds of our actions, thoughts, and dreams?"

Michael, his hands gently resting upon the mailbox, looked towards Tillie, seeing within her the boundless fields of tomorrow, "Indeed. Each thought we nurture, every deed we sow   is a seed, a prophecy, cast upon the winds of creation, destined to blossom wherever it may find purchase."

Gathering the letters within, they turned, beginning their gentle journey homeward, "In contemplating our own seeds, our own prophecies, a thought from the philosopher, Friedrich

Nietzsche, comes to heart. He reflected, 'He who has a why to live can bear almost any how.' Our seeds, our dreams, and hopes become our 'why,' guiding us through every 'how' we may traverse."

Tillie, the letters cradled in her arms, pondered upon her father's words, recognizing the infinite field of potential within each being, within every seed, thought, and action.

As father and daughter retraced their steps through the embrace of the warm summer day, the seeds of their reflections were cast upon the winds of their beings, becoming a part of the boundless, eternal field of creation, where each thought, action, and dream intertwines with all that is, was, and will be.

Note: Amidst the wisdoms of ancient prophecies and philosophical reflections, may we each recognize the infinite, creative potential within every moment, thought, and action, acknowledging our own role as both prophet and creator within the eternal dance of existence.

A Prayer

The divine Source of Wisdom enlightens our minds to perceive the patterns and principles that govern our existence. Bestow upon us the prophetic insight to foresee the consequences of our choices so that we may align ourselves more closely with your eternal laws. Guide us in heeding both your warnings and promises that we may navigate our lives toward hope, justice, and harmony. Amen.

Journaling Prompts

Reflect on a moment when you felt a deep sense of forewarning or foresight about a situation. How did this insight influence your actions, and what was the outcome?

1. Isaiah's prophecies involve both hope and warning. What are your own personal "prophecies" for your future—both the hopeful visions and the cautionary ones?

2. What spiritual or ethical principles guide you in making decisions about your future? Have these principles ever been in conflict with practical or societal pressures?

3. Describe a time when you ignored your inner "Isaiah," the intuitive part of you that foresaw consequences. What lessons did you learn?

4. In the context of today's social and political climate, which of Isaiah's themes (justice, peace, divine alignment) resonates most with you? Why?

Chapter Twenty
Daniel in the Lion's Den

Introduction

The story of Daniel in the lion's den is an iconic tale of faith triumphing over adversity. In the metaphysical lens, it serves as a study of the power of unshakeable trust and inner peace in the face of life's challenges.

Traditional Narrative

Daniel, an advisor to King Darius, is thrown into a lion's den for praying to God, defying a royal decree. His unwavering faith keeps him safe, and he emerges unscathed, leading to a decree honoring his God.

Biblical Context

This event occurred during the Babylonian exile, a time when the Israelites were far from their homeland and subjected to foreign rule. Daniel's faithfulness in such a setting speaks volumes about his spiritual integrity.

Interfaith and Cultural Perspectives

The narrative is revered in Jewish, Christian, and Islamic traditions alike, serving as a universal testament to the power of faith.

Metaphysical Interpretation

According to Charles Fillmore's Metaphysical Bible Dictionary, Daniel symbolizes the 'judgment faculty' in human consciousness. The lion's den represents the challenges or fears that test our spiritual convictions.

Quotes and References

Fillmore notes, "Daniel's safety amidst the lions symbolizes how unshakeable faith and inner composure can neutralize life's most threatening circumstances."

Real-world Examples

Think of situations where people have faced dire circumstances yet emerged unharmed or even strengthened, be it through courage, wisdom, or an inexplicable turn of events.

Practical Applications

Cultivating your own 'inner Daniel' involves practicing faith and discernment. When faced with challenges, rather than reacting impulsively, pause to align yourself with your core beliefs.

Reader Reflections

1. Have you ever been in a 'lion's den' situation? How did your faith or beliefs guide you?
2. What practices help you maintain inner composure during difficult times?

Concluding Thoughts

Daniel's experience in the lion's den illustrates that when we stand firmly in our spiritual truth, even seemingly insurmountable challenges can be overcome.

Glossary of Metaphysical Interpretations for This Chapter

- Daniel: Judgment faculty in human consciousness
- Lion's Den: Challenges or fears that test our faith
- King Darius: External authority that may conflict with inner spiritual law

- Royal Decree: Societal or external expectations that may contradict spiritual truths

Additional Exercises

1. A guided meditation focusing on building resilience and faith in the face of challenges.
2. Journaling prompts exploring past 'lion's den' moments and how you navigated them.

Chapter Twenty

Whispers Amidst the Rain, Faith Amidst the Den

The gentle pattering of raindrops on leaves and rooftops offered a soothing melody, enveloping Michael and his daughters, Tillie and Ellery, as they nestled into the comforting embrace of the front porch at Michael's mother's house. As droplets cascaded down, creating infinite ripples upon every surface they touched, they brought forth an ambiance of serenity and introspection.

Michael, his gaze journeying through the rain-washed world around them, turned towards his daughters, inviting them into a sacred space of reflection and sharing. "Girls, as we sit amidst this gentle summer rain, I find myself contemplating the tales and wisdoms of the past, and one, in particular, resonates at this moment."

Ellery, her eyes reflecting the dance of raindrops upon the world, inquired, "What story is it, Abba?"

The timbre of Michael's voice, soft amidst the serenade of the rain, carried forth the ancient tale, "It's the story of Daniel in the lion's den, a tale weaving through time from the ancient texts. Daniel, a man of unwavering faith, found himself condemned, cast into a den of lions for honoring his devotion to the Divine."

Tillie, her spirit dancing amidst the intertwining realms of story and reality, questioned, "Dad, how does one find such unshakable faith, even when facing the jaws of death?"

Michael, recognizing the profound depth of her inquiry, responded, "Tillie, faith, in its essence, resides beyond the realms of seen and unseen, known and unknown. It is a trust, a knowing, that within the infinite, there is benevolence, a divine order interwoven through all."

Taking a moment to embody the wisdoms within the tale, he continued, "Daniel, amidst the potential terror of the den, found serenity and communion with the Divine. His faith became a shield, and in that unwavering trust, the lions, too, found peace, and thus, he emerged unharmed."

Ellery, her thoughts entwined with the soothing caress of the rain, softly reflected, "Abba, it seems as if his faith transformed the nature of his reality, turning threat into ally and fear into love."

"Indeed, Ellery," Michael, his heart resonating with her reflection, shared further, "Charles Fillmore, in his metaphysical interpretations, saw the lions as symbolic of our own unrestrained thoughts and emotions. In perceiving them through faith, not as threats, but as aspects of the Divine, they transformed from peril into harmony."

The trio, enveloped by the gentle embrace of the rain, delved deeper into the reflections birthed from the tale, exploring the lions within their own beings and the faith that has the potential to transform fear into understanding and turmoil into peace.

In the gentle weaving of shared insights and ponderings, Michael, carrying forth a contemplation from the philosopher Søren Kierkegaard, shared, "Kierkegaard, a philosopher who delved deeply into the realms of faith, reflected, 'Faith is the highest passion in a human being. Many in every generation may not come that far, but none comes further.'"

As the words echoed amidst the symphony of the rain, Tillie, Ellery, and Michael explored the landscapes of their own faiths, recognizing the infinite dance of the Divine through every moment, thought, and interaction, acknowledging that within every challenge, within every 'lion's den,' there is the potential for profound trust and transformative faith.

Amidst the whispers of the rain and the ancient tales brought forth through the generations, they discovered the timeless echoes of wisdom and faith, recognizing that within each being, within every 'lion,' there resides a sacred communion with the Infinite, waiting to be recognized, honored, and embraced.

Note: As we journey through our own tales, may we, too, recognize the lions within our own dens and, through faith, transform them from perils into companions upon the path, discovering the harmonious dance of the Divine through all aspects of creation.

A Prayer

Eternal Protector, strengthen our faith and sharpen our discernment as we walk through the lion's dens of our lives. Infuse us with the unshakeable trust and inner peace that Daniel embodied. Help us to stand firm in our spiritual convictions, especially when faced with external challenges that test our inner resolve. In Your Name, we pray for the courage to remain steadfast. Amen.

Journaling Prompts

Describe a 'lion's den' moment in your life where you felt severely tested or challenged. What inner resources did you draw upon to navigate through it?

1. Think of a time when external pressures, symbolized by "King Darius" and his "Royal Decree," conflicted with your inner spiritual or ethical beliefs. How did you resolve this conflict?

2. What practices or rituals help you cultivate your 'inner Daniel,' enabling you to face challenges with faith and inner composure?

3. Have you ever experienced a miraculous turn of event akin to Daniel's miraculous survival? What do you attribute this to?

4. In facing life's challenges, do you find it more natural to rely on faith or on analytical judgment? Do you see a way for these two to coexist in your life?

Chapter Twenty-One
Jonah and the Whale

Introduction

The tale of Jonah and the whale is more than just a dramatic story of a man swallowed by a sea creature. It serves as a metaphysical exploration of obedience to divine guidance, personal transformation, and the consequences of avoiding one's spiritual path.

Traditional Narrative

Jonah is a prophet who attempts to evade God's instruction to warn the people of Nineveh about impending divine wrath. He boards a ship going in the opposite direction but is eventually swallowed by a whale. After three days and nights, he is spat out, leading him to fulfill his prophetic duty.

Biblical Context

The Book of Jonah is part of the Minor Prophets in the Hebrew Bible and is often considered more a story of personal transformation than a typical prophetic book focused on a nation's fate.

Interfaith and Cultural Perspectives

Jonah's ordeal transcends religious boundaries, appearing in Jewish, Christian, and Islamic texts. It universally resonates as a tale of avoiding and then accepting one's spiritual duties.

Metaphysical Interpretation

According to Charles Fillmore's Metaphysical Bible Dictionary, Jonah symbolizes the human aspect of consciousness that avoids spiritual growth or responsibility. The whale represents large challenges or circumstances that force us into transformation.

Quotes and References

Fillmore suggests, "The whale swallowing Jonah portrays how life's trials, often self-created, serve as catalysts for spiritual evolution and alignment with divine will."

Real-world Examples

Consider the instances where people avoid responsibilities, only to face even greater challenges that ultimately steer them back to their intended path.

Practical Applications

To awaken your 'inner Jonah,' become aware of any resistance you have toward embracing your spiritual duties. When faced with challenges, see them as opportunities for growth rather than punishments.

Reader Reflections

1. Can you recall a time when avoiding a responsibility led to unexpected challenges?
2. How did those challenges shape your spiritual or personal growth?

Concluding Thoughts

Jonah's story reminds us that evading our spiritual calling can lead to situations designed to propel us back onto our destined path. It serves as a cautionary tale and an inspirational guide to embracing our spiritual duties.

Glossary of Metaphysical Interpretations for This Chapter

- Jonah: Human consciousness avoiding spiritual growth
- Whale: Catalysts for forced transformation
- Nineveh: Conditions or people that require spiritual enlightenment
- Ship: Means of escape from spiritual responsibility

Additional Exercises

1. A guided meditation on embracing change and spiritual responsibilities.
2. Journaling prompts for reflecting on times you've avoided your spiritual or life's calling and how you were redirected back onto your path.

Chapter Twenty-One
Echoes of the Whale, Lessons from the Depths

The radiant summer sun bestowed its gentle warmth upon the expansive landscape of Dolan's Lake as Michael and his daughters, Ellery and Tillie, found themselves embraced by the beauty and tranquility of their surroundings. The soft caress of the summer breeze, interwoven with the gentle lapping of the water upon the shore, crafted an ambiance of serene reflection and connectedness.

As they ambled along the picturesque lake, the sacredness of nature enveloping them, Michael, turning towards his daughters, invited them into ancient tales and timeless wisdom. "Tillie, Ellery, amidst the beauty of this day, a story from of ancient teachings is calling to be shared and explored."

Tillie, her spirit always ready to delve into the realms of story and reflection, inquired with a gentle curiosity, "Which story is it, Dad?"

"It's the story of Jonah and the whale," Michael responded, his voice a soft echo amidst the natural symphony surrounding them. "Jonah, through his journey within the depths of the whale, brings forth profound insights into the nature of resistance, surrender, and redemption."

As the words flowed forth, intertwining with the gentle rustling of the leaves and the harmonic melodies of the birds, he shared the ancient tale. "Jonah, called by the Divine to venture to the city of Nineveh and convey a message of transformation and repentance, found resistance within his being and, thus, sought to flee from the calling. His attempt to escape led him into the belly of a great whale, within which he found himself immersed in the depths of contemplation and surrender."

Ellery, absorbing the resonance of the story amidst the beauty of their surroundings, reflected, "It seems, Abba, that the whale, rather than being a punishment, offered Jonah a sanctuary of reflection, an opportunity to delve into his own depths."

Michael, affirming her insights, expanded, "Yes, Ellery. In Charles Fillmore's metaphysical interpretation, the whale represents our own ability to delve into our inner depths to embrace the aspects of ourselves that we may resist or seek to flee from. Within the belly of the whale, in the embracing of our own inner depths, we discover the path of surrender and the unfolding of divine guidance."

As they continued their walk, the beauty of Dolan's Lake reflecting the infinite wisdom of nature around them, they explored the depths of their own beings, recognizing the 'whales' within their own lives and the gifts that arise from surrendering into the embrace of their own inner journeys.

Guided by the wisdom of the philosopher   Rumi, Michael shared, "Rumi, a poet and philosopher of profound depth and insight, once reflected accept what troubles you've been given, the door will open.' Within our own beings, within the acceptance and embracing of our own depths and challenges, we discover the doorways to understanding, transformation, and the unfolding of the Divine."

Nailed It

As Tillie, Ellery, and Michael, bathed in the radiant light of the summer sun and enveloped by the sacredness of Dolan's Lake, explored the echoes of Jonah's journey within their own paths, they recognized that within every moment of resistance, within every 'whale,' there is an invitation into deeper understanding, surrender, and the transformative power of divine guidance.

In the harmonious dance of nature, story, and reflection, they discovered the timeless wisdoms interwoven through every tale, every being, and every moment, recognizing the sacred journey of diving into the depths, emerging transformed through the embrace of surrender and the boundless ocean of divine love.

Note: Within our own stories, may we, too, find the courage to delve into our own depths, to surrender into the embrace of our own 'whales,' discovering the transformative power of acceptance and the unfolding of divine wisdom through every aspect of our beings and journeys.

A Prayer

Dear Divine Presence,

Guide us in our journey of spiritual growth and transformation. Help us to recognize when we are running from our responsibilities and our true calling. Give us the courage to face the "whales" in our lives, the challenges that push us toward our destined path.

May we learn, as Jonah did, that avoiding our spiritual duties only leads to greater trials. Help us to see these trials not as punishments but as opportunities to align ourselves more closely with Your divine will.

Grant us the wisdom to understand that sometimes life's detours are actually the path to our true selves. May we find strength in our "whale moments," using them as catalysts for growth and spiritual enlightenment.

Amen.

Journaling Prompts

Describe a moment in your life when you tried to avoid a spiritual or personal responsibility. What were the circumstances, and how did you feel?

1. Have you ever had a "whale moment " where life seemed to forcefully redirect you back to your intended path? What happened, and what did you learn?

2. How do you generally react when faced with challenges that you perceive as obstacles to your plans? Do you see them as punishments or as opportunities for growth?

3. In the story of Jonah, the people of Nineveh represent conditions or people that require spiritual enlightenment. Are there any "Ninevehs" in your life that you feel called to help or enlighten?

4. If Jonah symbolizes the human consciousness that avoids spiritual growth, what are some ways you can awaken your 'inner Jonah' to be more receptive to personal and spiritual transformation?

Part Two
The New Testament

Chapter One
The Nativity

Introduction

The Nativity is a cornerstone of Christian belief, but it also has metaphysical dimensions that are universally compelling. It speaks to the birth of divine consciousness within the human experience.

Traditional Narrative

The birth of Jesus is foretold by an angel to Mary, a virgin who is conceived by the Holy Spirit. She and her husband, Joseph, travel to Bethlehem, where Jesus is born in a manger because there's no room at the inn.

Biblical Context

The Nativity story is found mainly in the Gospels of Matthew and Luke. Each offers different details, but the core message remains the same: the divine made manifest in human form.

Interfaith and Cultural Perspectives

The birth of Jesus is recognized not just in Christianity but also in Islam and other faiths, albeit with varying interpretations and levels of significance.

Metaphysical Interpretation

According to Charles Fillmore's Metaphysical Bible Dictionary, the birth of Jesus symbolizes the awakening of Christ's consciousness within us. Mary and Joseph represent purity and righteous will, essential for birthing new spiritual awareness.

Quotes and References

Fillmore writes, "The Nativity story is a roadmap for individual spiritual unfoldment, a guide to birthing the divine within."

Real-world Examples

The birth of a child often catalyzes personal transformation for parents, marking a shift in responsibilities and a deepening of love and selflessness, akin to spiritual awakening.

Practical Applications

To nurture your 'inner Mary and Joseph,' cultivate purity of thought and righteousness of action. In doing so, you prepare the 'manger' of your heart for higher spiritual consciousness.

Reader Reflections

1. What has catalyzed spiritual 'births' or awakenings in your own life?
2. How can you prepare your inner 'manger' for new spiritual growth?

Concluding Thoughts

The Nativity is not just a historical or religious account; it's a living metaphor for spiritual awakening, a guide for manifesting the divine within us.

Glossary of Metaphysical Interpretations for This Chapter

- Mary: Purity and divine receptivity

- Joseph: Righteous will and intention

- Jesus: Christ's consciousness

- Bethlehem: 'House of Bread,' symbolizing spiritual sustenance

- Manger: Humble conditions suitable for spiritual birth

Additional Exercises

1. A guided meditation focusing on birthing new spiritual awareness within you.

2. Journaling prompts on identifying 'Mary and Joseph' qualities in yourself and how you can nurture them.

Chapter One
New Beginnings and Sacred Illuminations - The Nativity

The vast horizon of St. Louis unfolded gracefully before Michael and Ellery as the sprawling landscape of the Arch Park and the gentle flow of the river created a vibrant tableau full of life and unfolding possibilities. Their loft, perched on the sixth floor, offered a vantage point from which the pulsating life of the city and the tranquility of the natural world met in harmonious interplay. It was April, a time of renewal and burgeoning life, as they navigated through the myriad boxes and belongings, laying the foundation for their new chapter in this bustling metropolis.

Amidst the physical activity of organizing and settling, there lingered a palpable energy of reflection, a silent invitation to delve into the realms of deeper understanding and sacred wisdom. Michael, always interweaving the realms of daily life with the infinite, turned towards Ellery, an ancient tale glistening in his eyes, ready to emerge through the fabric of their current transition.

"Ellery," Michael began, his voice a gentle ripple amidst the subtle movements of their new abode, "within our journey here, within this new beginning, I'm reminded of another commencement, a story that holds the essence of purity, divine birth, and infinite possibility – The Nativity."

Michael shared, "In the story of the Nativity, we witness the birth of Jesus, a manifestation of pure consciousness, divine principle, born unto the earthly realm. This event, held within a humble stable amidst the creatures of the earth, carries within it profound symbology and metaphysical insight."

In Charles Fillmore's metaphysical interpretation, the birth of Jesus is not merely a historical event but a symbolic representation of the birthing of Christ's Consciousness within every individual. The stable, often perceived as lowly or ordinary, symbolizes the physical, the human experience within which the divine emerges and is recognized. Each character – Mary, Joseph, the shepherds, the Magi – embodies specific qualities and aspects of our own inner realms and our collective journey towards spiritual awakening and realization.

"Mary, embodying purity and divine receptivity, represents the intuitive aspect of our being, that which is open to receiving the divine impulse," Michael elucidated, "and Joseph, embodying strength, protection, and stable grounding, symbolizes the rational, logical aspect of our consciousness. Together, they create a sacred space, within which the Christ Consciousness, symbolized through Jesus, can be born, recognized, and nurtured."

The shepherds, embodying humility and simplicity, are often the first to recognize this divine emergence, symbolizing our own innate capacities to witness and honor the divine within when we approach with a heart of humility and genuine seeking. The Magi, traversing vast distances, guided by the Star of Bethlehem, embody the wisdom, devotion, and recognition of the sacred that resides within all and the journey that all beings are on, consciously or unconsciously, towards the realization of this sacredness.

Immersed in the unfolding depths of the story, Ellery pondered, "So, Dad, the Nativity isn't just about a singular event, but about recognizing the eternal birth of divine consciousness within us and all beings?"

"Precisely, Ellery," Michael affirmed, "It's a continuous, omnipresent unfolding, an eternal birth that is available and occurring within every moment, every being, and every situation."

As they pondered this, Michael, finding resonance with the philosophies held closely within his heart, shared Rumi a philosopher who explored deeply the realms of understanding, morality, and metaphysical truth once stated, "The journey of the soul is endless, as it seeks and finds the divine in all aspects of life, revealing that within every moment and every place lies an opportunity for rebirth and deeper connection with the universe." The Nativity, in its multifaceted symbology and depth, mirrors this, inviting us to recognize the awe-inspiring divinity within and all around us."

Within their new loft, amidst the boxes and the nascent forming of their new chapter in St. Louis, Michael and Ellery discovered a sacred space, a stable, within which they, too, could honor, nurture, and embody the Christ Consciousness, the divine principle, within their own beings and journey.

In the sacredness of the ordinary, amidst the moving boxes and the earthly realms of beginnings, they recognized the eternal birth of the divine, the infinite possibilities that arise when the spiritual and physical dance in harmonious union, and the sacred journey towards recognizing, nurturing, and embodying the divine consciousness within.

Note: The Nativity, in its eternal symbology and unfolding, invites us all to recognize, honor, and embody the divine birth that is continuously occurring within our own beings and journey, to navigate through our own stables with reverence, humility, and an open heart, and to witness the sacred, the divine, within the simplicity and profundity of every moment, every being, and every beginning.

A Prayer

Divine Spirit of All Creation,

In the quiet of my heart, I seek to understand the profound lessons of the Nativity. As the story of Jesus' birth unfolds, let it be a mirror reflecting the divine birth within my own soul. May the qualities of Mary's purity and Joseph's righteousness flourish in me, creating a sacred space for spiritual awakening.

Guide me to recognize the eternal Christ Consciousness that resides within all beings. As I journey through life's stables and stars, grant me the wisdom to see Your divine presence in every encounter and experience.

Help me nurture this inner divine spark with love, compassion, and humility, transforming my everyday moments into a living Nativity. May this sacred consciousness grow within me, guiding my thoughts, words, and actions toward greater love and understanding.

Every breath, in every step, reminds me of the continuous birth of divine consciousness that is my true nature and purpose.

Amen.

Journaling Prompts

1. **Reflection on Personal Nativity:** Think about moments in your life that felt like a 'divine birth' – a time when new understanding, compassion, or perspective emerged within you. How did these moments change you?

2. **Inner Mary and Joseph:** Reflect on how you embody the qualities of Mary (purity and receptivity) and Joseph (righteous will and intention) in your daily life. How do these qualities help in nurturing your spiritual growth?

3. **Recognizing the Christ Consciousness:** Contemplate instances where you have recognized or could recognize Christ's Consciousness in others or in the world around you. How does this recognition impact your interactions and perceptions?

4. **Embracing Humility and Simplicity:** Consider the role of humility and simplicity in your spiritual journey. How do these traits help you connect with the divine within and around you?

5. **The Star of Bethlehem in Your Life:** What represents the 'Star of Bethlehem' in your life – a guide or sign that leads you to deeper spiritual understanding? How do you follow this star, and what has it revealed to you?

Chapter Two
Jesus' Baptism and Temptation

Introduction

The baptism and subsequent temptation of Jesus serve as a profound template for the stages of spiritual initiation and challenges that follow. Through a metaphysical lens, these events echo the universal human experiences of spiritual awakening and testing.

Traditional Narrative

John the Baptist baptizes Jesus in the Jordan River, and the Holy Spirit descends upon Him like a dove. Soon after, Jesus is led into the wilderness by the Spirit and is tempted by Satan but resists successfully.

Biblical Context

The accounts of Jesus' baptism and temptation are crucial early events in the Gospels, setting the stage for His public ministry. They highlight the approval from the Divine ("This is my beloved Son") and the immediate challenges that follow.

Interfaith and Cultural Perspectives

While baptism is a predominantly Christian sacrament, the idea of ritual cleansing and spiritual testing exists in many religious traditions, emphasizing the universal aspects of these experiences.

Metaphysical Interpretation

In Charles Fillmore's Metaphysical Bible Dictionary, baptism represents the cleansing and renewal of the mind. The temptation in the wilderness symbolizes the ego's resistance to spiritual transformation.

Quotes and References

Fillmore mentions, "The descent of the Holy Spirit at baptism is akin to the intuitive insights and higher guidance we receive during moments of spiritual awakening."

Real-world Examples

A person going through a transformative life change—like a career shift or the loss of a loved one—often experiences moments of clarity followed by challenges that test their newfound perspective.

Practical Applications

After a spiritual awakening, symbolized by baptism, it's crucial to be vigilant against the ego's resistance, much like Jesus' temptation. Ground yourself in your spiritual practices to withstand the tests that will inevitably come.

Reader Reflections

- Have you experienced a 'baptism' or cleansing moment in your life?
- What 'wilderness' temptations have you faced after such transformative experiences?

Concluding Thoughts

Jesus' baptism and temptation are milestones that each seeker may encounter on the spiritual journey. They serve as reminders that moments of enlightenment are often followed by tests of faith and commitment.

Glossary of Metaphysical Interpretations for This Chapter

- Baptism: Spiritual cleansing and renewal
- Temptation: Egoic resistance to spiritual growth
- Jordan River: Flow of life force or spiritual energy
- Holy Spirit: Divine intuition and guidance

Additional Exercises

1. A guided meditation on experiencing spiritual cleansing and fortifying against temptations.

2. Journaling prompts on your own moments of spiritual awakening and the challenges that followed.

Chapter Two

On Lofted Heights - Baptism and Temptation

Under a sky that kissed the world with its vast, encompassing embrace, Michael, Ellery, and Tillie found themselves atop their loft, the sizzle of grilling chicken, imbued with aromatic herbs, wafting through the gentle breeze. The city's rhythm quietly hummed beneath them as they lofted above, nestled in a tranquil pocket of shared presence and connectivity.

As the St. Louis Arch majestically stretched into the heavens before them, Michael felt an inward nudge, gently steering their evening's discourse toward a pivotal moment – the baptism and temptation of Jesus.

Peering into the cascading sunlight that danced upon the distant river, Michael began, "Jesus' baptism and subsequent temptation in the wilderness offer a deeply symbolic and transformative lens through which we might explore our own spiritual unfolding."

Charles Fillmore, the co-founder of Unity, interpreted these events metaphysically, not as isolated historical occurrences, but as symbolic representations of stages within our own spiritual awakening and development.

"The baptism," Michael continued, gently turning the grilling chicken, "represents a cleansing, a purification, and an affirmation of the divine within us. John the Baptist symbolizes that within our consciousness which is preparing, making way, for a fuller realization and expression of our inherent divinity."

Ellery, intently absorbing each word, contemplated, "So, the baptism is like recognizing and embracing the divine within us?"

Michael nodded, "Indeed, Ellery. It's an inward affirmation, a conscious recognition and alignment with our divine nature. The Spirit descends like a dove, signifying the gentle, peaceful embrace of our divine identity, activating deeper aspects of our spiritual potential."

The three of them paused, allowing the profundity of that understanding to percolate through their being, merging with the all-encompassing view of the horizon where urban life and nature harmoniously converged.

"And then, the temptation," Michael added after a quiet moment, "comes forth as a necessary stage within our spiritual evolution. It symbolizes our encounters with the various facets of human experience - material desire, egoic power, and misaligned usage of our divine faculties."

He looked at his daughters, their expressions thoughtful, and found a quote from Joseph Campbell echoing through his mind, "We must be willing to let go of the life we planned so as to have the life that is waiting for us."

"This idea," he continued, "is reminiscent of the temptations faced by Jesus in the wilderness. He navigated through the illusions of power, materiality, and misalignment, emerging with an unwavering alignment with his divine identity and purpose."

Tillie, with her ever-curious gaze, queried, "Is the temptation, then, a kind of test for our spirit, Dad?"

"In a way, Tillie," Michael responded, "It's an integral aspect of our journey, where our alignment with, and understanding of, our divine nature is explored and expressed through our human experience. These experiences invite us to embody, with every thought, word, and action, the divine qualities and understanding we have realized within."

As the grilled chicken, perfectly cooked and infused with herbs, was placed atop fresh, vibrant salads, the trio, on that elevated rooftop, found themselves simultaneously grounded and uplifted within a space where spiritual insights, symbolic stories, and the palpable, loving connection between them coalesced into a sacred moment of being.

The tales of baptism and temptation, when viewed through a metaphysical lens, became not merely stories from a distant past but a living, breathing narrative, ever-relevant and deeply intertwined within their own stories, journeys, and unfolding realizations.

And so, they dined beneath the vast sky amidst the rhythmic

hum of the city, enveloped in a tangible serenity, where stories of old and present moments intertwined, guiding, illuminating, and eternally whispering of the divine presence, forever dancing within and all around.

Note: As we delve into the stories of the past, seeing through a metaphysical lens, we find that they are not just tales of distant figures and times but symbolic narratives, ever-relevant, whispering eternal truths and guiding our own spiritual journey and awakening within the here and now.

A Prayer

Ever-Present Divine Light,

As I reflect upon the baptism and temptation of Jesus, guide me in my own journey of spiritual awakening and resilience. May the waters of baptism cleanse my thoughts and renew my spirit, preparing me for the divine purpose you have set for me.

In moments of temptation, when the ego and material desire cloud my path, grant me the strength and wisdom to discern and choose the higher way. Help me to recognize these challenges as opportunities for growth, strengthening my commitment to my spiritual path.

Fill me with the grace of the Holy Spirit so that I may remain steadfast in my journey, embodying the qualities of purity, righteousness, and divine alignment. May I rise from each test with a deeper understanding and a stronger connection to my inner divine essence?

Guide me to live a life that reflects the lessons of Jesus' baptism and temptation, embracing each day as an opportunity for spiritual deepening and service to others.

Amen.

Journaling Prompts

1. **Personal Baptism Experience:** Reflect on a moment in your life that felt like a spiritual baptism, a cleansing or awakening. How did this experience change your perspective or actions?

2. **Facing Temptations:** Consider a time when you faced a temptation or challenge following a significant spiritual or personal awakening. How did you handle it, and what did you learn about yourself?

3. **Symbolism of Water in Your Life:** Water often symbolizes cleansing and renewal. Write about an experience where water (a river, rain, ocean, etc.) played a significant role in your spiritual or emotional journey.

4. **Egoic Resistance:** Identify moments when your ego resisted spiritual growth or change. How did you recognize this resistance, and what steps did you take to overcome it?

5. **Divine Guidance**: Recall instances where you felt divinely guided or inspired, akin to the descent of the Holy Spirit during Jesus' baptism. How did this guidance manifest, and what impact did it have on your life?

Chapter Three
The Sermon on the Mount

Introduction

The Sermon on the Mount is one of the most famous teachings in all of religious and philosophical literature. Its metaphysical significance lies in its comprehensive blueprint for attaining higher spiritual consciousness.

Traditional Narrative

Jesus delivers this sermon to a multitude on a mountainside. It encompasses teachings like the Beatitudes, the Golden Rule, and the Lord's Prayer, providing ethical and spiritual guidelines for living.

Biblical Context

Found in the Gospel of Matthew, chapters 5–7, this sermon has been seen as both revolutionary and timeless, offering wisdom that transcends cultural and religious boundaries.

Interfaith and Cultural Perspectives

The principles in the Sermon on the Mount have parallels in many spiritual traditions, emphasizing virtues like compassion, humility, and the pursuit of inner purity.

Metaphysical Interpretation

Charles Fillmore's Metaphysical Bible Dictionary suggests that the mountain represents the highest state of consciousness attainable. The sermon, therefore, is spiritual instruction for those aspiring to reach this elevated state.

Quotes and References

Fillmore states, "The Sermon on the Mount is a manual for achieving Christ consciousness, a roadmap to the higher self."

Real-world Examples

Ethical business leaders who prioritize employee well-being and corporate responsibility often embody principles found in the Sermon on the Mount.

Practical Applications

To apply the teachings of the Sermon in your life, practice mindful living, focusing on being rather than doing, on the inner world rather than external achievements.

Reader Reflections

1. Which teaching from the Sermon on the Mount resonates most with you?
2. How do you implement these spiritual teachings in your daily life?

Concluding Thoughts

The Sermon on the Mount is not just a set of moral guidelines but a call to elevate one's consciousness, an invitation to live from the highest self.

Glossary of Metaphysical Interpretations for This Chapter

- Mountain: The highest state of spiritual consciousness
- Beatitudes: Qualities of the awakened soul
- Lord's Prayer: Blueprint for spiritual connection and daily living

- Golden Rule: Universal principle of ethical reciprocity

Additional Exercises

1. A guided meditation on embodying the Beatitudes in your daily life.

2. Journaling prompts exploring how you've experienced or practiced the teachings of the Sermon on the Mount.

Chapter Three
Walking Through Teachings - The Sermon on the Mount

The vibrant energy of the summer pulsed through the city of St. Louis as Michael, Ellery, and Tillie embarked on a leisurely walk from their loft toward the iconic Gateway Arch. Sunlight bathed the streets, creating a canvas where shadows and light danced in an ephemeral play, mirroring the dynamic interplay of everyday life and deeper truths.

Through the labyrinth of streets and structures and the seamless merging of nature with the urban landscape, they found themselves collectively immersed in a tranquil bubble, where the external world softly faded, giving way to a shared space of exploration and reflection.

Michael, perceiving the natural flow of their connection, began to weave into their journey a tale of teachings, humility, and profound wisdom - The Sermon on the Mount.

"Ellery, Tillie," Michael began, with a gentle cadence, "Today, as we meander through our own path, I'm reminded of a moment in time, embedded with timeless teachings, spoken softly upon a mount – The Sermon on the Mount."

Jesus, amidst the gentle embrace of nature, elevated upon a mount, spoke to those gathered and to generations beyond, embedding within his words profound truths and universal principles. "Blessed are the meek, for they shall inherit the earth," Jesus proclaimed, inviting all beings into a space of humility, gentleness, and genuine connection with the sacredness of life.

In Charles Fillmore's metaphysical lens, The Sermon on the Mount is perceived not merely as moral directives but as profound, spiritual insights into the nature of being and the path towards realizing the kingdom of heaven within.

"The mount," Michael illuminated, "is symbolically representative of a state of elevated consciousness, a space within us that is of a higher vibrational frequency, where our perception expands into the realms of unity, love, and divine wisdom."

"'Blessed are the pure in heart, for they shall see God,'" Michael quoted, "It speaks to the inner purity, the essence of our being that is unblemished, eternal, and inherently connected with the Divine. To 'see' God is to recognize, realize, and embody the Divine within our own being and in all of existence."

As they approached the arch, its magnificence drawing shadows and light upon the grass, Tillie reflected, "So, the blessings and the teachings aren't about seeking external rewards, but about recognizing and embodying the truths and the divine qualities within us?"

Michael nodded, "Exactly, Tillie. The Beatitudes, and indeed the entirety of the Sermon on the Mount, invite us into a journey inward, to explore, embody, and express the qualities – meekness, purity, mercy, peace – within our own consciousness and being."

Under the expansive arch, which seemed to graciously unite the earth and the heavens, they found a silent space of reflection, each of them pondering the teachings, the blessings, and the infinite expressions of the divine encapsulated within every aspect of life.

Ellery, gazing upon the arch and then softly towards Michael, shared, "Dad, it feels as though every moment, every interaction, is an invitation to recognize and embody these teachings, to navigate through life with an open heart, a pure intent, and a conscious being."

In an echo of assent, Michael responded, "Indeed, Ellery.

The journey is perpetual, an eternal dance where we are continuously invited to embody, explore, and express the divine qualities within us. The wisdom shared in the Sermon on the Mount is not bound to a specific time or place but is alive, resonant within every heartbeat, every breath, and every moment of connection."

As the trio lingered under the arch, the teachings of the Sermon on the Mount quietly interweaving with their own reflections, stories, and shared moments, there was a silent yet profound recognition of the sacredness, the divinity, embedded within every aspect of their journey, their being, and the eternal now.

And thus, amidst the grandeur of the arch and the simplicity of their shared presence, they found the kingdom of heaven within, gently unfolding, endlessly expansive, and eternally present.

Note: In the teachings of the Sermon on the Mount, we are all invited into a space of reflection, embodiment, and conscious living, where the qualities of the divine are not distant or separate but are inherent within our being, our journey, and every moment of life. Through humility, purity, and genuine connection, we navigate through the landscapes of life, continuously exploring, recognizing, and expressing the divine within.

A Prayer

O Divine Wisdom,

As I reflect upon the profound teachings of the Sermon on the Mount, guide my heart and mind to embrace these timeless truths. Let the Beatitudes be a compass in my life, guiding me toward humility, mercy, and purity of heart.

Instill in me the courage to live by the Golden Rule, treating others with the kindness and respect I seek for myself. Help me to embody the essence of the Lord's Prayer, fostering a relationship with You that is deep, personal, and transformative.

Grant me the wisdom to see the sacred in the ordinary, to find blessings in challenges, and to cultivate an inner peace that withstands the trials of life. May my actions reflect the higher consciousness that Jesus taught on the mount.

In every moment, let me be an instrument of Your love, spreading light and compassion in a world in need of healing and understanding.

Amen.

Journaling Prompts

1. **Living the Beatitudes:** Choose one Beatitude that particularly resonates with you. Reflect on how you can actively embody this quality in your daily life.

2. **The Golden Rule in Action:** Recall a recent situation where you applied (or could have applied) the Golden Rule. How did it impact your interaction and your feelings about the situation?

3. **Personal Reflection on the Lord's Prayer:** Write about what the Lord's Prayer means to you personally. How do its words guide you in your spiritual journey?

4. **Challenges and Blessings:** Reflect on a challenging time in your life. How did this experience bring about spiritual growth or blessing in line with the teachings of the Sermon on the Mount?

5. Applying the Sermon's Teachings Identify a specific teaching from the Sermon on the Mount and write about how you can integrate this teaching into your everyday life.

Chapter Four
Miracles of Jesus

Introduction

The miracles performed by Jesus are captivating not just for their supernatural elements but also for their metaphysical implications. They serve as living metaphors for the transformative power of faith and divine consciousness.

Traditional Narrative

Jesus performs numerous miracles during his ministry, including healing the sick, turning water into wine, and feeding thousands with a few loaves and fish.

Biblical Context

These miraculous events are scattered across the four Gospels, each symbolizing different aspects of divine intervention and the breaking of natural laws for a higher purpose.

Interfaith and Cultural Perspectives

Miracles, or extraordinary events attributed to divine agency, are found in various religious and spiritual traditions, underlining the universal allure of the miraculous.

Metaphysical Interpretation

In Charles Fillmore's Metaphysical Bible Dictionary, the miracles signify the outworking of spiritual laws that transcend the limitations of material laws. For instance, healing the blind signifies inner illumination, while feeding the masses symbolizes spiritual abundance.

Quotes and References

Fillmore notes, "Jesus' miracles are not just acts of compassion but instructional demonstrations of how divine laws operate in the realm of human experience."

Real-world Examples

Modern-day 'miracles,' such as spontaneous remission from severe illness or unexpected acts of kindness, can be viewed as expressions of underlying spiritual principles.

Practical Applications

Cultivate your inner faith and understanding of spiritual laws to invite 'miraculous' changes in your life. Believe in the power of positive thought, compassion, and divine guidance.

Reader Reflections

1. Have you experienced or witnessed what you would call a 'miracle'?
2. How do you reconcile the miraculous with your understanding of natural laws?

Concluding Thoughts

The miracles of Jesus are not just extraordinary events but illustrative examples of spiritual laws in action, pointing us toward greater understanding and application of these principles.

Glossary of Metaphysical Interpretations for This Chapter

- Healing: Spiritual wholeness and alignment
- Multiplication of food: Spiritual abundance
- Turning water into wine: Transformation and elevation of consciousness

- Walking on water: Mastery over emotional turbulence

Additional Exercises

1. A guided meditation on inviting 'miraculous' changes through faith and understanding.
2. Journaling prompts about experiences that have seemed 'miraculous' and what spiritual principles they might represent.

Chapter Four

Metro Musings - The Miracles of Jesus

June's sun cast its gentle, golden hue upon St. Louis, tracing a path of light and shadows on the streets. Michael, Ellery, and Tillie, their spirits tinted with anticipation, found themselves amidst the hum of the city, on the platform awaiting the metro that would whisk them toward the renowned Anheuser Busch Stadium.

The platform was a mosaic of life, where diverse paths intersected for a moment. A few individuals, perhaps cast adrift by life's tumultuous currents, lingered, their presence weaving a thread of ambiguity into the fabric of the day.

Ellery, observant and empathetic, leaned toward Michael, her voice a hushed whisper, "Dad, do you ever think about the stories behind the eyes of those who seem lost or troubled?"

Michael nodded, his gaze gently meeting those around them, "Indeed, Ellery, beneath the surface of every soul lies a depth of stories, struggles, joys, and sorrows, often unseen but ever-present."

As the metro slid into the station, the trio boarded, finding a space where they could engage in thoughtful discourse amidst the rhythmic motion of their journey.

Amidst the ambient sounds of conversations, the distant city, and the steady clatter of the metro, Michael found a bridge to their next reflection, "Speaking of the unseen and the miraculous, it brings to mind the miracles performed by Jesus as depicted in the New Testament."

Tillie, her curiosity piqued, chimed in, "What do the miracles tell us, Dad? What can we learn from them today?"

With a thoughtful pause, Michael began, "Charles Fillmore offered a metaphysical interpretation of Jesus' miracles, viewing them not merely as historical events but as symbolic representations of the transformative power and potential within each of us."

He continued, "Take, for instance, the miracle of turning water into wine. Metaphysically, water might be seen as representing the unformed substance of the divine, and wine is a symbol of realization and manifestation. The miracle suggests a transformation from potentiality into actuality – an awakening and manifesting of latent divine capacities within."

As the metro navigated through the urban landscape inside, a journey of spiritual exploration unfolded.

Ellery, contemplating, shared, "So, it's like Jesus was showing us our own potential to bring forth, or manifest, love, healing, and abundance in our lives by aligning with that divine essence within us?"

Michael warmly affirmed, "Precisely, Ellery. Each miracle, from healing the sick to feeding multitudes, symbolizes aspects of our own spiritual capacities and evolution. They invite us to recognize and activate the divine potentials that dwell inherently within us – to be co-creators in our world, bringing forth healing, abundance, and harmony through our aligned thoughts, words, and actions."

The metro, in its steady course, mirrored their conversational journey – a moving through physical and metaphysical landscapes, exploring the stories and symbols that whisper of the transcendent and imminent divine interwoven within every moment and every soul.

As they neared their destination, Michael, embracing the day, his daughters, and the journey, shared a quote by William Blake, "If the doors of perception were cleansed, everything would appear to man as it is, infinite."

With that, they stepped forth from the metro, hearts and minds ever-expanding, into an afternoon where tangible experiences and spiritual insights would continue to weave a web of deeper understanding and interconnectedness. Their journey through the streets toward the stadium became yet another beautiful stage where life's miracles, seen and unseen, continuously unfolded around and within them.

Note: The miracles, seen through the metaphysical lens, become not only tales of wonder from times past but also symbolic narratives, inviting us to recognize, realize, and express the divine capacities and potentials that inherently dwell within us here and now.

A Prayer

Divine Essence of All That Is,

As I ponder the miracles of Jesus, open my heart and mind to the miraculous in my own life. Teach me to see beyond the physical realm and recognize the spiritual significance in everyday events.

Help me cultivate a deep faith akin to the faith that fueled these miracles so I might witness and partake in the extraordinary hidden within the ordinary. Guide me to understand the metaphysical meanings behind these miraculous events, seeing them as symbols of the transformative power of divine consciousness.

Inspire me to embody the principles of love, compassion, and abundance so that I might be a living testament to the miraculous potential within each of us. Grant me the wisdom to see life's challenges as opportunities for growth and manifestation of Your divine law.

May my life be a reflection of these miracles, a testament to the boundless possibilities when aligned with Your spiritual laws.

Amen.

Journaling Prompts

1. **Recognizing Miracles:** Reflect on an event in your life that you consider a miracle. What made it miraculous, and how did it impact your beliefs or perspective?

2. **Inner Transformation:** Consider a personal transformation you have experienced that felt miraculous. What inner changes did it involve, and how did it affect your life?

3. **Manifesting Miracles:** Write about a situation where you wish to see a 'miraculous' change or improvement. How can you align your thoughts and actions with spiritual principles to facilitate this change?

4. **Lessons from Jesus' Miracles:** Choose one miracle performed by Jesus and explore its metaphysical symbolism. How does this symbolism apply to your life or spiritual journey?

5. **Faith in Action:** Reflect on how your faith or belief system has played a role in experiencing or understanding miracles. How does faith shape your perception of the possible and the impossible?

Chapter Five
The Parables of Jesus

Introduction

The parables of Jesus are deceptively simple stories packed with profound spiritual lessons. Through a metaphysical lens, these tales are not just moral guidelines but transformative spiritual principles.

Traditional Narrative

Jesus frequently taught through parables like the Good Samaritan, the Prodigal Son, and the Parable of the Sower, often using everyday scenarios to impart heavenly wisdom.

Biblical Context

Found mainly in the Synoptic Gospels (Matthew, Mark, and Luke), these parables are aimed at conveying complex spiritual truths in a manner accessible to everyone.

Interfaith and Cultural Perspectives

Parables or allegorical stories appear in many religious traditions as a pedagogical tool, emphasizing universally acknowledged virtues and life lessons.

Metaphysical Interpretation

According to Charles Fillmore's Metaphysical Bible Dictionary, each parable encapsulates spiritual laws or states of consciousness. For instance, the Parable of the Sower deals with how different states of human consciousness receive spiritual truth.

Quotes and References

Fillmore states, "The parables are a mirror reflecting the innermost spiritual conditions and aspirations of every individual."

Real-world Examples

A modern interpretation of the Good Samaritan could be acts of unconditional kindness in today's divided social climate, serving as real-world examples of spiritual principles in action.

Practical Applications

Recognize the spiritual laws or principles presented in the parables and apply them in daily life. For instance, be the 'good soil' that effectively receives and nurtures the 'seeds' of wisdom and love.

Reader Reflections

1. Which parable of Jesus resonates most with you, and why?
2. How do you see these parables applying in today's world?

Concluding Thoughts

The parables are more than stories; they are spiritual equations describing the dynamics of the soul's journey toward divine consciousness.

Glossary of Metaphysical Interpretations for This Chapter

- Good Samaritan: Unconditional love and compassion
- Prodigal Son: The soul's return to divine origin
- Parable of the Sower: Consciousness and receptivity to spiritual truth
- Talents: Divine endowments and their right use

Additional Exercises

1. A guided meditation focusing on becoming the 'good soil' in the Parable of the Sower.
2. Journaling prompts exploring how you've applied the lessons from Jesus' parables in your daily life.

Chapter Five

Morning Meanderings - The Parables of Jesus

On a serene summer morning, the rising sun gilded the Mississippi, casting reflections upon its gentle ripples. The arch, a sentinel of St. Louis, watched over the awakening city, its curved form becoming aglow with the first light. Michael and Ellery stepped into the unfolding day, embarking on their cherished morning walk from the loft toward their favorite sanctuary of aroma and warmth – the downtown coffee shop.

Streets were alive with a symphony of urban life: the rhythmic pattering of joggers' feet, soft murmurs of early risers in conversation, and the distant, gentle hum of the waking city. The milieu provided a perfect canvas upon which father and daughter would inscribe their morning reflections.

"Ellery," Michael began, his voice softly riding the gentle breeze, "the parables of Jesus, as explored through the lens of Charles Fillmore's metaphysical interpretations, unveil deeper insights into our own spiritual journey and potential."

Ellery, absorbing the tranquility of the morning, responded, "I recall some of the parables, Dad. They've always intrigued me with their simplicity yet profound messages. How does Fillmore explore them metaphysically?"

Michael, looking ahead where the light delicately painted the edges of the city, initiated the discourse, "Let's ponder upon the Parable of the Sower, where a sower scatters seeds upon various types of soil. Each type of soil, metaphysically, represents different states of our consciousness and receptivity to the Word – the divine ideas and truths."

As they strolled through the peaceful streets, the metaphor of the seeds found resonance in the nature that permeated even this urban environment - trees lining the streets and patches of green, each hosting seeds once sown, now manifested in myriad forms of life.

"The seed falling on the path, which is not able to sprout, symbolizes when divine ideas are not understood or taken to heart, they cannot take root within our consciousness," Michael elucidated. "The seed upon rocky ground, which sprouts quickly but then withers, mirrors our temporary and surface-level engagements with spiritual ideas that do not permeate deeply into our being."

Navigating through their path, they witnessed myriad interactions of city-dwellers with their environment – some strolling mindfully, others rushing, oblivious to the blossoms and bird songs around them.

"And the seed sown among thorns, which are choked as they try to grow," Michael continued, "represents how worries, materialism, and external distractions can stifle our spiritual growth."

Ellery, connecting the metaphor to lived experiences, noted, "So, the different types of soil are akin to our varied states of mind and heart, and how they determine our capacity to understand, embrace, and manifest divine truths in our lives."

Michael nodded, his gaze gentle upon his daughter, "Indeed, and the seed in good soil - that which brings forth grain, growing and multiplying - symbolizes when we receive, embody, and proliferate divine ideas from a state of understanding, openness, and alignment."

Nailed It

A quote by George Bernard Shaw subtly wove itself into Michael's narrative, "The gardener does not create the garden; the garden creates the gardener."

As they neared the coffee shop, the aroma of freshly ground beans whispered promises of warmth and wakefulness. Ellery, pondering deeply, queried, "Is there another parable you find particularly profound, Dad?

Michael, as they stepped into the welcoming embrace of the coffee shop, began to delve into the Parable of the Prodigal Son, "This parable symbolizes our human journey of separation and return. The prodigal son, seeking to experience life independently of his father, squanders his inheritance only to find himself in destitution. In his suffering, he realizes the abundance and love ever-present in his father's house and decides to return."

With coffees in hand, they found a cozy nook, and amidst the gentle hum of morning conversations, Michael elucidated, "Metaphysically, the prodigal son's journey symbolizes our own ventures into material consciousness - seeking fulfillment and identity outside of our divine source, only to realize, often amidst challenges, that true abundance, love, and wholeness are found in our return to spiritual awareness and alignment."

He added, with a gentle smile, a thought from Rumi, "What you seek is seeking you." Michael mused, "In our wanderings, like the prodigal son, we may realize that what we were seeking in external experiences and material pursuits is found within - the love, acceptance, and abundance of the divine, ever-present, ever-seeking our return to awareness and unity."

With hearts warmed by both coffee and reflection, Michael and Ellery, gazing through the window at the city now bathed in the full light of morning, allowed the parables to seep into their beings like the morning light that gently permeates every crevice of the world, illuminating, awakening, and transforming.

Note: Engaging with the parables metaphysically invites us to explore and reflect upon our own spiritual journey, consciousness, and evolution, recognizing the deeper truths, teachings, and potentials embedded within these timeless narratives and within ourselves.

A Prayer

Divine Teacher,

As I delve into the parables of Jesus, imbue me with the wisdom to understand their deep spiritual meanings. Let these stories illuminate the path of my own spiritual journey, revealing truths that guide and transform.

Grant me the insight to see beyond the literal narrative to the profound principles they represent. Help me to internalize the lessons of the Good Samaritan, the Prodigal Son, the Parable of the Sower, and others, allowing them to shape my thoughts, actions, and interactions with others.

May these parables inspire me to cultivate a heart of compassion, a spirit of forgiveness, and a life that bears the fruit of spiritual understanding. Let them be a constant reminder of Your presence and guidance in every aspect of my life.

In my daily endeavors, may I embody the virtues these parables teach, becoming a living example of the divine truths they convey.

Amen.

Journaling Prompts

1. **Personal Reflection on a Parable:** Choose one of Jesus' parables that particularly speaks to you. Reflect on its deeper meaning in your life and how you can apply its lessons.

2. **Modern-Day Good Samaritan:** Consider how you can be a 'Good Samaritan' in today's world. What are some practical ways you can show compassion and kindness to those around you?

3. **Learning from the Prodigal Son:** Reflect on a time when you, like the Prodigal Son, ventured away from your core values or beliefs. What did you learn from this experience, and how did it bring you back to your spiritual center?

4. **The Parable of the Sower in Your Life:** Identify which type of soil (path, rocky ground, thorns, or good soil) you currently embody in your spiritual journey. How can you cultivate your inner 'good soil' to better receive and nurture spiritual truths?

5. **Applying Parables to Personal Challenges:** Think of a current challenge or situation in your life. How can the teachings from one of Jesus' parables provide guidance or a new perspective on this challenge?

Chapter Six
Jesus and the Samaritan Woman

Introduction

The encounter between Jesus and the Samaritan woman is a lesson in breaking social norms for the sake of spiritual enlightenment. Metaphysically, it touches on themes of inclusion, transformation, and the quest for living water or spiritual sustenance.

Traditional Narrative

Jesus meets a Samaritan woman at a well. Despite cultural taboos, he speaks with her and offers her "living water," revealing his identity as the Messiah.

Biblical Context

This story occurs in the Gospel of John, chapter 4. It stands out for crossing boundaries of gender, religion, and ethnicity, thereby emphasizing the universality of spiritual truths.

Interfaith and Cultural Perspectives

The idea of crossing boundaries to attain spiritual wisdom is a common theme in many religious and spiritual traditions, reinforcing the universal importance of inner transformation over external divisions.

Metaphysical Interpretation

According to Charles Fillmore's Metaphysical Bible Dictionary, the well symbolizes traditional religious or intellectual concepts, while "living water" symbolizes the higher, spiritual understanding that Jesus offers.

Quotes and References

Fillmore notes, "The Samaritan woman represents a state of consciousness open but still bound by traditional beliefs. The living water is the Christ consciousness that frees one from such limitations."

Real-world Examples

Consider social activists who cross societal boundaries to address human needs, embodying the spiritual principle of universal love and inclusion seen in this story.

Practical Applications

Reflect on your own "wells" or traditional beliefs that may limit your spiritual growth. Seek the "living water" of a higher, inclusive consciousness that transcends these limitations.

Reader Reflections

1. Have you ever crossed a social or cultural boundary for a greater understanding or experience?
2. What do you think is the "living water" in your life?

Concluding Thoughts

The story of Jesus and the Samaritan woman serves as an inspiring example of how spiritual understanding can transcend social and cultural boundaries, inviting us to elevate our own states of consciousness.

Glossary of Metaphysical Interpretations for This Chapter

- Well, Traditional religious or intellectual concepts
- Living Water: Spiritual wisdom or enlightenment

- Samaritan Woman: Consciousness that is open but traditionally bounded
- Messiah: The Christ's consciousness or divine wisdom within

Additional Exercises

1. A guided meditation on identifying and transcending your own limiting beliefs or "wells."
2. Journaling prompts focused on experiences where you felt spiritually limited and how you can seek "living water."

Chapter Six

Divinity by the River - Jesus and the Samaritan Woman

On a sun-dappled summer day, Michael, Ellery, and Tillie found themselves on the graceful slopes of a Grafton, Illinois winery, overlooking the grandeur of the river below, its waters gently narrating tales of distant lands. Amidst the vine-laden terraces, the trio sought both physical and spiritual refreshment, meandering through the lush vines and partaking of the earthly delights the winery bestowed.

With a glass of crimson richness cradled gently in his hand, Michael began to unspool the tale of Jesus and the Samaritan woman, his voice drifting amidst the vines, inviting contemplation.

In a harmonious blend of Charles Fillmore's metaphysical interpretations and the soothing environment, he began, "The meeting of Jesus and the Samaritan woman at the well, Ellery, Tillie, is more than a historical tale. It symbolizes an inner dialogue, a meeting between our higher self (Jesus) and our striving, seeking self (the Samaritan woman)."

Tillie, with eyes reflecting the expansive sky, questioned, "What were they seeking, Dad? Why did Jesus talk to her when it was unusual for Jews and Samaritans to speak to each other?"

A gentle breeze whispered through the vines as Michael explained, "The Samaritan woman represents our soul's yearning and seeking for something deeper, more sustaining – living water, or spiritual sustenance. She had been drawing physical water, which could quench physical thirst, but was seeking something to quench her deeper, spiritual thirst."

He added, considering the wine in his hand, "Much like we enjoy this wine, which brings a transient joy and relaxation, our souls seek a more perpetual, deeper satisfaction and unity, which is symbolized by the living water Jesus speaks of."

The sun gently caressed the vineyard, highlighting the vibrancy of the grapes, each cluster a testament to the nourishment derived from both earth and heavens, an embodiment of union and fruition.

Ellery, observing the parallel, noted, "So, the physical water, or the wine here, represents our earthly joys and pleasures, while the living water Jesus offers represents an eternal, spiritual fulfillment and connection."

Exactly," Michael affirmed, "Jesus' dialogue with the Samaritan woman invites us to explore our own inner dialogues, our own seeking of deeper, spiritual truths and connections amidst our earthly experiences and pursuits."

The river below, in its perpetual flow, mirrored the eternal living waters of spiritual wisdom and connection, ever-present, ever-flowing, ever-available, inviting them to partake, to be quenched, to be renewed.

Michael, imbuing the narrative with a quote from the philosopher Pierre Teilhard de Chardin, shared, "We are not human beings having a spiritual experience. We are spiritual beings having a human experience."

He elucidated, "Our encounters with earthly joys, pleasures, and challenges, much like the Samaritan woman's engagements and struggles, are part of our human experience. But beneath, or rather, within it all, we are spiritual beings, and our deeper yearning is for that eternal, spiritual 'water' – the connection, unity, and embodiment of divine love and wisdom."

The vineyard, in its splendid isolation, became a sanctuary where earthly and spiritual met, where the physical fruits of the vine symbolized the inner fruits of the spirit, each sip inviting reflection upon the deeper, eternal quenching offered by spiritual communion.

As the sun dipped towards the horizon, casting long shadows upon the verdant landscape, Michael, Ellery, and Tillie lingered, allowing the parable to seep into their beings to mingle with their own experiences, yearnings, and inner dialogues.

Tillie, with a thoughtful gaze upon the river, mused, "The living water is always there, isn't it, Dad? In every moment, every experience, it's inviting us to connect, to drink, to be fulfilled."

Michael, placing a gentle arm around Tillie, responded, "Absolutely, Tills. It's in every sunrise, every grape turned to wine, every moment shared with loved ones. It's the undercurrent of divine love and wisdom in our lives, inviting us to recognize, embrace, and be transformed by it."

In the tranquility of the vineyard, amidst the vines and beneath the expansive sky, they found a moment of communion – with each other, with the earth, and with the eternal, living waters that course through every aspect of being, inviting, always inviting, to partake, to be quenched, to be united.

And so, as the physical day gave way to night, the spiritual light within them, illuminated by the parable, remained an eternal flame, ever-burning, ever-offering warmth and light upon their paths.

Note: The metaphysical interpretation invites us to delve deeper into the symbolic, spiritual meanings and implications of Biblical narratives, exploring how they mirror, represent, and invite our own spiritual understanding, growth, and evolution.

The Wellspring of transformation

Act 1: a tale of Perception and possibility.

The sun blazed down from a cloudless sky, casting a golden veil over the arid landscape. The Traveler, his robes dusted by the desert and his sandals scuffed by the miles he had covered, approached a well located on the outskirts of a small Samaritan village. He felt the weight of his journey in every step, the ground beneath him hot and unforgiving, almost as if the Earth itself were weary.

As he came closer, he noticed the Samaritan Woman already at the well, her form outlined against the shimmering air. She stood there, a simple figure in a worn but vibrant gown, her hair pulled back in a cloth to shield it from the relentless sun. Her hands were calloused but firm, gripping a coarse rope attached to a wooden pulley. The creaking of the pulley and the splashing of water broke the afternoon's silence as she drew the liquid treasure up from the depths below.

The Traveler paused, watching her for a moment before speaking. "May I have a drink?" he inquired, his voice tinged with a deep fatigue but also an unspoken wisdom.

The Samaritan Woman hesitated, her eyes narrowing slightly as they met his. They were eyes that had seen hardship and days too long under the sun, yet they sparkled with a quiet resilience.

She was about to hand him a ladle of water, her skepticism apparent, yet something held her back.

Sensing her reluctance, The Traveler chose his next words carefully, "Wouldn't you like to have water that grants everlasting life instead?" His eyes seemed to peer into her very soul, challenging her to look beyond the obvious, to delve into a realm that transcended the tangible.

For a moment, their eyes locked, two worlds colliding. Hers, a life led through the five senses, limited yet comfortable in its familiarity. His existence, unfettered by such boundaries, invites her to step into a transformative unknown.

The air between them thickened with tension and curiosity, laying the groundwork for an exchange that would challenge the very core of their beings. And so, with this encounter, their fates were irrevocably entwined, setting the stage for an odyssey into the wellspring of human consciousness.

Act 2: The Five Husbands

The Samaritan Woman looked at The Traveler, her eyes a mix of intrigue and guarded skepticism. "Everlasting life, you say?" Her voice conveyed a muted excitement tinged with disbelief, like a child who has been told a fantastical tale but is not sure whether to buy into the magic. "My life has been tethered to reality by my five husbands," she declared, emphasizing the word 'five' as if each syllable carried the weight of a lifetime.

In saying 'five husbands,' she wasn't speaking of marital bonds but of the five senses that had shaped her understanding of the world—sight, sound, taste, touch, smell. These were her reliable companions, yet also her jailers, limiting her experiences to what could be quantified and qualified. Her eyes conveyed the struggle, a flicker of yearning obscured by the fog of doubt.

The Traveler looked at her knowingly, his gaze unflinching as if he saw through the veil that shrouded her true self. "And the one you're with now isn't your husband," he said softly, almost whispering, as a gentle breeze rustled the leaves of a nearby olive tree.

The implication of his words hung in the air like a delicate perfume, both alluring and unsettling. He was telling her that her present state of consciousness, grounded as it was in sensory perception, was not her authentic self. It was as though he had unlocked a hidden door within her, pointing to a space that she had neglected or perhaps never even knew existed.

For a brief moment, the Samaritan Woman felt as if the ground beneath her had shifted. The well, the rope in her hand, and even the air she breathed seemed momentarily unreal, like props on a stage. The Traveler's words had sown a seed of unsettling thought: Could it be that her entire understanding of life, anchored by her five senses, was but a shadow of something far greater?

It was a disquieting notion, and yet it carried an irresistible allure. The words of The Traveler had carved a question into her soul, a question that would serve as the turning point for her journey inward, toward the realm of the unfathomable.

Act 3: The Living Water

The air seemed to hold its breath as The Traveler fixed his gaze on the Samaritan Woman, who stood frozen in contemplation. "Worship what you know," he began, his voice imbued with a soothing yet compelling authority. Each word emanated from him like a ripple on a placid pond, quietly disturbing the surface yet leaving no trace of its passage.

His statement served as an invitation as much as a challenge. It urged her to forsake her reliance on her five senses, the 'five husbands,' and reach into the depths of her own inner world. "Taste the living water," he continued, gesturing toward the well beside them, "and awaken the dormant power of your imagination."

The term 'living water' was enigmatic, yet it resonated within her as if she had heard it before, perhaps in a long-forgotten dream. In that instant, she understood it to be a metaphor for a transformative force, a creative power that lay within her, waiting to be tapped. This living water was her imagination unbound, a font of potential that could rewrite the story of her existence.

The Samaritan Woman looked at the well beside her, its familiar stonework and wooden structure suddenly taking on a new significance. She realized it was not just a well of earthly water but a symbolic reservoir of her subconscious, where her beliefs, fears, and aspirations resided like hidden treasures or lurking shadows.

It was a critical moment, a juncture where she could either turn back to the familiarity of her sensory world or take a step into the unknown. The decision loomed before her, both exciting and terrifying, and the weight of it momentarily crushed her with indecision.

But as she met The Traveler's eyes once again, something within her shifted. There was an undeniable sincerity in his gaze, an unspoken promise that the journey, though fraught with uncertainty, would lead to a revelation beyond her wildest imaginings.

In that fleeting moment, a new sense of resolve rose within her, pushing her past her hesitations and uncertainties.

Act 4: The Transformation

Summoning her newfound courage, the Samaritan Woman hesitantly reached for the ladle that lay beside the well. Her hand trembled slightly as she submerged it into the water, now understanding that this simple act was laden with symbolic weight. With a sense of awe, she lifted the ladle to her lips and tasted the water.

As the cool liquid touched her tongue, an electric sensation surged through her as if she had swallowed a draught of pure, unfiltered consciousness. The world around her blurred and refocused in sensations and insights, both familiar and astonishingly new. The rough texture of the rope in her hand, the distant chirping of a bird, and even the warmth of the sun above her—all melded into an intricate symphony that went beyond her five senses.

For the first time, she found herself viewing reality not merely through the narrow lens of sensory perception but through the expansive eye of imagination. The limitations of her 'five husbands' fell away, revealing a landscape rich with possibilities, where the mundane transformed into the miraculous and where her own thoughts and beliefs manifested as vivid experiences.

"Go, call your husbands and come back," said The Traveler, his voice echoing as if from a great distance and yet intimately near. His words were an enigmatic instruction, a command to integrate this newfound realm of perception into her everyday life. To live not as a prisoner of her five senses but as a liberated being imbued with the creative power of her own imagination.

As she looked at The Traveler, her eyes now luminous with a light of their own, she understood that he had not bestowed this transformation upon her but had merely acted as a guide, leading her to discover the wellspring of potential within herself.

She nodded, a silent affirmation of her commitment to this new path,

Act 5: The New Paradigm

The Samaritan Woman returned to her village, her steps infused with a newfound purpose and her heart beating to a rhythm of transformation. Her eyes, once vessels of mere sight, were now windows to a soul awakened, capturing not just the forms and colors of her surroundings but the essence that lay beneath.

As she walked through the narrow, bustling streets of her village, her fellow villagers noticed something different about her— a radiance, a sense of calm that seemed almost otherworldly. The everyday chatter, the clatter of pots and pans, and the laughter of children all seemed to resonate with deeper meanings and melodies in the magnificent symphony of existence.

Gathering her community around her, she spoke of The Traveler and the living water, her voice imbued with a conviction that only comes from direct experience. She told them of her transformative encounter at the well, the well of consciousness, where she had tasted water that was not just a sustenance for the body but nourishment for the soul.

Her words, both simple and profound, split the crowd into believers and skeptics. Some dismissed her story as the ramblings of a woman touched by the sun's heat, while others sensed the truth in her words and felt their hearts stir with curiosity and hope.

Those who chose to believe asked her to lead them to the

well. And there, following her example, they, too, tasted the living water. As they did, expressions of awe and wonder spread across their faces. They had also stepped into the realm of the imaginative, the realm of possibility, where the limitations of the five senses were transcended by the limitless scope of creative thought.

The story of the Samaritan Woman and The Traveler spread throughout the village and beyond, a tale of liberation from the constraints of sensory perception and an invitation to explore the untapped reservoirs of the subconscious mind. Not everyone took the plunge into this new paradigm, but those who did found their lives irrevocably changed, their realities reshaped by the transformative power of imagination and belief.

A Prayer

Divine Source of Living Water,

As I reflect on the story of Jesus and the Samaritan woman, guide me to embrace the lessons of inclusion, understanding, and spiritual nourishment. Help me to break down the walls of prejudice and division, just as Jesus did, and to see the divine spark in every person I encounter.

Instill in me a thirst for the living water of spiritual wisdom. May I seek this higher understanding with an open heart and mind, transcending my own limitations and traditional beliefs.

Grant me the courage to cross the boundaries of my comfort zone in pursuit of deeper spiritual truths. Let me be a conduit of Your love and acceptance, reaching out to those who are different from me with compassion and empathy.

In my own quest for spiritual growth, help me to find and share the living water that refreshes the soul and brings true fulfillment and unity with Your divine presence.

Amen.

Journaling Prompts

1. **Breaking Social Norms for Spiritual Growth:** Reflect on a time when you broke a social or cultural norm to gain a greater understanding or experience. What did you learn, and how did it impact your spiritual journey?

2. **Seeking 'Living Water' in Your Life:** What does the concept of 'living water' mean to you? How do you seek this spiritual sustenance in your daily life?

3. **Learning from the Samaritan Woman:** Identify with the Samaritan woman's journey. What traditional beliefs or limitations are you holding onto, and how can you transcend them for greater spiritual understanding?

4. **Inclusion and Empathy:** Consider how you can practice inclusion and empathy in your interactions inspired by Jesus' conversation with the Samaritan woman. How can this practice enhance your spiritual growth?

5. **Transformative Encounters:** Think of an encounter that had a significant impact on your spiritual beliefs or practices. What was transformative about this experience, and how did it change you?

Chapter Seven
The Transfiguration

Introduction

The Transfiguration of Jesus is a mysterious and awe-inspiring event that serves as a powerful symbol of spiritual elevation and divine manifestation. Through a metaphysical lens, it represents the transformative power of attaining higher states of consciousness.

Traditional Narrative

Jesus takes Peter, James, and John to a mountain where he is transfigured before them. His face shines like the sun, and his clothes become dazzlingly white. Moses and Elijah appear beside him, and a voice from a cloud proclaims, "This is my Son, whom I love; with him I am well pleased."

Biblical Context

The Transfiguration occurs in all three Synoptic Gospels (Matthew 17:1–9, Mark 9:2–8, Luke 9:28–36), serving as a pivotal moment that reveals Jesus's divine nature and mission.

Interfaith and Cultural Perspectives

The notion of human-to-divine transformation is a common motif in various religious and mythological traditions, emphasizing the potential for spiritual ascension.

Metaphysical Interpretation

In Charles Fillmore's Metaphysical Bible Dictionary, the mountain symbolizes the high state of spiritual consciousness. The appearance of Moses and Elijah represents the Law and the Prophets, respectively, and their integration into the Christ Consciousness.

Quotes and References

Fillmore observes, "The Transfiguration serves as an example of how the individual, having mastered certain spiritual laws, can elevate the whole being into divine light."

Real-world Examples

Personal moments of "transfiguration," such as life-changing spiritual experiences or realizations, reflect the inner potential for divine transformation within us all.

Practical Applications

Strive to attain higher states of spiritual consciousness through meditation, prayer, and understanding of spiritual laws, allowing your own form of transfiguration to unfold.

Reader Reflections

1. Have you experienced a moment of "transfiguration" or profound spiritual insight in your own life?
2. What do the figures of Moses and Elijah symbolize for you in your spiritual journey?

Concluding Thoughts

The Transfiguration not only confirms Jesus's divine identity but also demonstrates the possibility of human transcendence into higher realms of spiritual understanding.

Glossary of Metaphysical Interpretations for This Chapter

- Mountain: Elevated state of spiritual consciousness
- Moses and Elijah: Law and Prophets integrated into Christ Consciousness
- Dazzling White: Purity and divine wisdom

- Cloud: The overshadowing divine presence

Additional Exercises

1. A guided meditation focusing on elevating your state of consciousness.

2. Journaling prompts you to explore moments when you've felt close to a state of "transfiguration" in your own life.

Chapter Seven
Radiance Amongst the Rocks - The Transfiguration

The rolling wheels of Michael's car came to a gentle halt on the dust-laden path of the River Road adjacent to the renowned Pisces bird cave in Alton. There, enveloped by a summer day's embrace, Ellery, Tillie, and Michael embarked on an exploration rich not only with the physical beauty of their surroundings but permeated with a spiritual profundity that transcended the rocky terrains of the cave.

As the trio tread gently upon the path leading to the cave, the melody of distant birds adorning the serene summer sky, Michael began to weave the tale of the Transfiguration of Jesus, his voice a gentle caress amidst the natural symphony surrounding them.

"In a realm high upon a mountain, Jesus was transfigured into a being of radiant light, revealing his divine nature to Peter, James, and John," Michael began, his eyes reflecting the rich, verdant landscapes around them. "This moment, girls, was a glimpse into the divine essence residing within the physical manifestation of Jesus."

The entrance of the Pisces cave loomed ahead, a shadowy contrast to the sunlit path behind them. Its rocky walls whispered ancient tales, and within its cool, dimly lit depths, they found a juxtaposition of light and shadow, a metaphor that enhanced the unfolding narrative.

Tillie, with curiosity illuminating her eyes, queried, "So, Dad, does the light that shone from Jesus represent something more, something we can't always see?"

Michael nodded, guiding them gently into the cave, where beams of sunlight pierced through crevices, creating pockets of illumination amidst the shadows. "Indeed, Tillie. The light represents the inherent divinity within Jesus – an essence of absolute love, wisdom, and power. Charles Fillmore suggests that this divine light resides within us all, albeit often shrouded by our physical, earthly experiences and perceptions."

Navigating through the rugged, shadowy contours of the cave, Michael continued, "The Transfiguration is a symbolic narrative inviting us to recognize and allow our own inner light – our innate divinity – to shine forth, transcending the shadows of our fears, doubts, and limiting beliefs."

Ellery, absorbing the intertwining of the narrative and their environment, reflected, "It's like these beams of light in the cave, isn't it, Dad? They find their way through the tiniest gaps, illuminating the darkness, revealing the beauty hidden within the shadows."

"Yes, Ellery," Michael responded, pausing to allow a beam of light to caress his features, "Our inner divine light, too, seeks expression, seeking avenues through our thoughts, words, and deeds to illuminate, to love, to heal, and to guide, not only our own paths but to light the way for others too."

As they explored further, the shadows within the cave deepening, yet ever punctuated by threads of light, Michael infused the narrative with a philosophical reflection, sharing an idea inspired by Jung's philosophy: "The meeting of two personalities is like the contact of two chemical substances: if there is any reaction, both are transformed."

Expanding upon the words, Michael shared, "Our journey towards recognizing and expressing our inherent divinity is deeply personal and subjective. Like the disciples, we might witness expressions of divine light in myriad forms, but it is within our own beings that we must discover, nurture, and allow our unique expression of that divine essence to radiate."

The cave, with its intricate dance of light and shadow, bore silent witness to their exploration, both physical and metaphysical.

Emerging from its depths, back into the embrace of the sunlit world outside, they carried with them not just an exploration of rocky terrains but an inner exploration of the divine terrains within themselves.

There, amidst nature, they lingered, allowing the tales of ancient texts and the wisdom of philosophical thought to mingle with their own lights, ever-present, ever-waiting to pierce through the shadows, to illuminate, to transfigure, and to reveal the radiance within.

The exploration of the Transfiguration through metaphysical eyes invites a personal reflection upon our own potential for transformation, illumination, and the expression of our innate divinity. And in that sacred space of reflection, we find the beams of our own lights, seeking, always seeking, to shine forth, to love, to heal, and to unite.

A Prayer

Divine Light of Transformation,

As I contemplate the Transfiguration of Jesus, inspire me to seek my own spiritual elevation. Help me to ascend the metaphorical mountains in my life, striving for higher states of consciousness and closer communion with You.

Guide me in understanding the profound symbolism of this event – the radiant light, the presence of Moses and Elijah, and the divine voice from the cloud. Let these symbols be a beacon on my path to spiritual enlightenment.

Encourage me to embrace transformation in my life, shedding the limitations of my lower self to reveal the divine essence within. May I be transfigured in spirit, radiating Your love and wisdom in all that I do.

In moments of doubt or struggle, remind me of the possibility of transcending the mundane to experience Your divine presence. May I be an embodiment of Your light, shining brightly in a world in need of spiritual truth.

Amen.

Journaling Prompts

1. **Personal Transfiguration Moments:** Reflect on moments in your life that felt like a personal transfiguration – times when you felt a profound spiritual shift or insight. What triggered these moments, and how did they transform you?

2. **Symbolism of Moses and Elijah:** Consider what Moses and Elijah might symbolize in your spiritual journey. What do they represent to you, and how do their teachings influence your path?

3. **Aspiring to Higher Consciousness:** Write about the 'mountains' you are currently climbing in your quest for higher consciousness. What challenges and insights are you encountering on this ascent?

4. **Embodying Divine Light:** How can you strive to embody the divine light witnessed in the Transfiguration in your daily life? What practical steps can you take to radiate this light to others?

5. **Voice from the Cloud:** Imagine hearing a divine voice as in the Transfiguration. What message would you hope to receive, and how would it guide your current spiritual path?

Chapter Eight
The Last Supper and Betrayal

Introduction

The Last Supper and the subsequent betrayal of Jesus mark a turning point in the New Testament narrative. From a metaphysical standpoint, they represent the struggle between spiritual growth and material entanglements.

Traditional Narrative

Jesus shares a final meal with his disciples, foretelling his betrayal by one of them. Later, Judas Iscariot betrays Jesus to the authorities for thirty pieces of silver.

Biblical Context

This poignant episode appears in all four Gospels, emphasizing its importance in the Christian narrative as the prelude to Jesus's crucifixion and resurrection.

Interfaith and Cultural Perspectives

Betrayal and sacrifice are themes that resonate across multiple religious and cultural traditions, revealing deep psychological and spiritual complexities.

Metaphysical Interpretation

According to Charles Fillmore's Metaphysical Bible Dictionary, the Last Supper symbolizes the feeding of spiritual substance to our inner faculties, while the betrayal highlights the conflict between spiritual aspirations and worldly temptations.

Quotes and References

Fillmore suggests, "The betrayal by Judas represents how the worldly-oriented mind can mislead the spiritual faculties, leading to suffering but also eventual awakening."

Real-world Examples

Instances where personal ambition or material gain have led to ethical compromises can be viewed as modern-day analogs to the betrayal by Judas.

Practical Applications

Reflect on moments when you've faced the pull between your higher spiritual self and materialistic or ego-driven desires. Use such experiences as stepping stones for spiritual growth.

Reader Reflections

1. Can you identify a "Judas" moment in your life when you felt betrayed by your own choices?
2. How do you feed your "inner disciples" with spiritual substance?

Concluding Thoughts

The Last Supper and Betrayal serve as cautionary yet enlightening events that challenge us to maintain spiritual integrity even when faced with worldly temptations.

Glossary of Metaphysical Interpretations for This Chapter

- Last Supper: Feeding spiritual substance to inner faculties
- Betrayal: Conflict between spiritual and material orientations
- Thirty Pieces of Silver: Material gains that are superficial

and short-lived

- Disciples: Inner faculties that can be nurtured or misled

322

Additional Exercises

1. A guided meditation focusing on balancing spiritual and material concerns.
2. Journaling prompts exploring moments of conflict between spiritual values and material temptations.

Chapter Eight

Moonlit Reflections on Betrayal and Unity - The Last Supper and Betrayal

The glow of a full moon caressed the nighttime canvas above St. Louis, weaving a the night with a gentle, contemplative ambiance. Ellery and Michael, with hearts entwined in the confluence of spiritual growth and paternal bond, found themselves nestled within a quaint Mexican restaurant downtown, vegetarian choices abounding, and a pitcher of margaritas serving as a fluid companion to their forthcoming discourse.

As Michael sipped thoughtfully upon his margarita, the chilled glass whispering of a summer's night's ease, he broached the poignant tale of the Last Supper and the ensuing betrayal that painted the final earthly days of Jesus with unity and treachery.

"Ellery," Michael began, the weight of the narrative gently shadowing his expression, "the Last Supper, as articulated in the Bible, transcends a mere gathering. It becomes a symbiotic space where love and betrayal, unity and separation, divinely entwine."

The tantalizing aroma of vegetarian dishes wafted through the air as they delved deeper into the narrative. Michael continued, "Within that sacred space, Jesus shared bread and wine, symbolizing his body and blood, offering sustenance and unity to those gathered, even as the shadow of betrayal lingered."

Ellery, her gaze alight with introspective reflections, considered the juxtaposition. "It's such a paradox, Dad. Offering love and unity, even in the face of betrayal. It speaks of such a profound, unconditional love, doesn't it?"

"Yes, E," Michael responded, his voice a gentle affirmation amidst the ambient murmur of diners around them. "Charles Fillmore interprets the Last Supper metaphysically as a symbolic representation of our capacity to internalize and express the Christ Consciousness – to embody love, forgiveness, and wisdom, even in the midst of challenges and betrayals."

As they nourished their bodies with a meal rich in flavors yet devoid of harm to sentient beings, they explored further the metaphysical dimensions of the tale.

"The bread and wine," Michael explained, "can be seen as symbols of our innate abilities to absorb and express divine substance and life. Even amidst the shadows of Judas' betrayal, Jesus symbolically offered, and continues to offer, sustenance, love, and unity to all."

The moon, a silent observer in their celestial ceiling, cast a gentle glow upon the streets of St. Louis as they stepped outside, the narrative weaving through their thoughts beneath the celestial canvas above.

Michael, enveloping the moment within a philosophical context, shared a quote from Mahatma Gandhi: "The enemy is fear. We think it is hate, but it is fear."

Exploring the depths of the words, Michael reflected, "In the face of betrayal, in the spaces where fear resides, there too, we find an invitation to illuminate, to love, and to transcend. For within every act that seeks to diminish the light, there resides a cry for love, a hunger for illumination, and in recognizing this, we, like Jesus, can offer love amidst the shadows."

They walked side by side, the streets bathed in moonlight and reflection, where tales of love and betrayal, unity and separation, danced in celestial harmony, inviting them to perceive, to illuminate, and to love, even amidst the shadows, even amidst the betrayals.

And there, beneath the gentle gaze of the moon, Ellery and Michael found a silent unity, a sacred communion, where words became superfluous, and their hearts spoke in silent.

The Last Supper and betrayal, invite contemplation upon our own capacities to love, forgive, and shine forth, even when shadows cast their transient veils upon our paths. Thus, in the sacred spaces of our beings, we find the Christ within, ever beckoning, ever illuminating, even amidst the darkened corridors of fear and betrayal.

Chapter Nine
The Crucifixion and Resurrection

Introduction

The Crucifixion and Resurrection stand as the climax of the Christian narrative, embodying themes of sacrifice, redemption, and transcendence. In metaphysical terms, they illustrate the transformative journey of the soul through trials to ultimate liberation.

Traditional Narrative

Jesus is crucified between two criminals, asking God to forgive those who have wronged him. Three days later, he rises from the dead, appearing to Mary Magdalene and later his disciples, signifying the defeat of death and sin.

Biblical Context

These events are recounted in all four Gospels and form the cornerstone of Christian belief, capturing the paradox of tragedy and triumph, human frailty and divine power.

Interfaith and Cultural Perspectives

The theme of death and rebirth is ubiquitous across various religious traditions, symbolizing the cyclical nature of life and the prospect of spiritual renewal.

Metaphysical Interpretation

According to Charles Fillmore's Metaphysical Bible Dictionary, the Crucifixion represents the purging of lower egoic tendencies, while the Resurrection signifies the soul's ascendancy into a new state of spiritual consciousness.

Quotes and References

Fillmore writes, "The Crucifixion and Resurrection are not just historical events but eternal spiritual principles, guiding the soul through its evolutionary journey."

Real-world Examples

Life crises that lead to transformative personal growth are modern instances of the crucifixion and resurrection process.

Practical Applications

Embrace life's challenges as opportunities for spiritual growth, knowing that each "crucifixion" phase is a precursor to a "resurrection" in consciousness.

Reader Reflections

1. Can you recall a "crucifixion" moment in your life that led to significant personal or spiritual growth?
2. How do you conceptualize the idea of "resurrection" in your own spiritual journey?

Concluding Thoughts

The Crucifixion and Resurrection offer profound metaphysical insights into the human condition, encouraging us to transcend our limitations and reach for higher states of spiritual awakening.

Glossary of Metaphysical Interpretations for This Chapter

- Crucifixion: The purging of lower egoic tendencies
- Resurrection: Ascendancy into higher spiritual consciousness

- Three Days: The period of transition and transformation
- Mary Magdalene: The intuitive aspect that first recognizes the new spiritual state

Additional Exercises

1. A guided meditation on letting go of limiting beliefs and embracing spiritual rebirth.
2. Journaling prompts you to explore your own cycles of "death and rebirth" in life experiences.

Chapter Nine
Transcending Shadows - The Crucifixion and Resurrection

The click of the front door announced Michael's unexpected return, startling in the midday silence. Ellery, awash with a maelstrom of emotion, her senses instantly alert, anticipated a disturbance in their ordinary life. The typical workday had shattered into something unrecognizable as Michael, with eyes darkened by the shadow of his own tumult, stepped across the threshold, not as the rock of the family but as a man under a palpable burden.

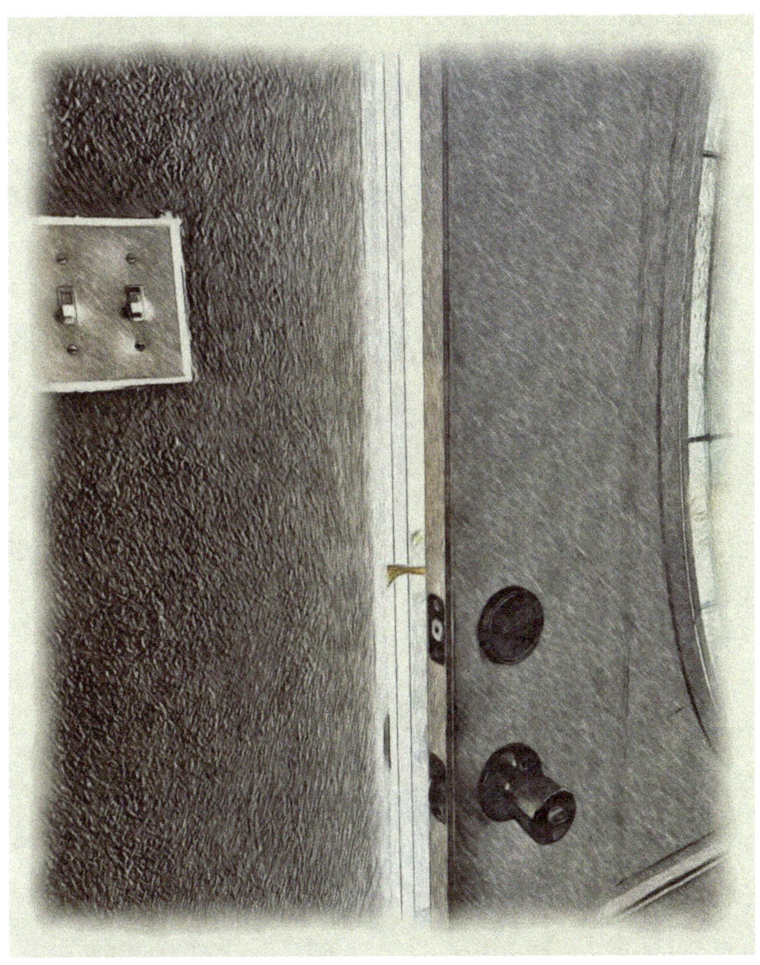

Ellery's heart winced as she met his gaze, recognizing the fragility often shrouded beneath layers of stoic strength. The aura of turmoil wavered about him as Michael confessed, with a voice choked by the battle between shame and vulnerability, "I got fired today, Ellery."

Moments suspended between them, delicate and taut, as

Ellery grappled with the undulating waves of disappointment, empathy, and fear for the future. Here, amid the fragments of a disrupted reality, she recalled the narratives of crucifixions and resurrections – stories of decay and rebirth, darkness and light, endings and beginnings.

Summoning the strength embedded within tales of transcendence and redemption, Ellery invited Michael on a walk. Side by side, yet distanced by the encroaching shadows, they treaded upon familiar paths, now rendered alien by the specter of uncertainty and the scorching pain of betrayal - of Michael to his responsibilities and to himself.

"Dad," Ellery whispered, the wind carrying her words as an offering, not of condemnation but of unconditional love, "the crucifixion and resurrection story in the Bible isn't merely a historical event to ponder. It's a metaphorical journey which we all traverse in various shades and moments in our lives."

The path beneath their feet, once solid, now seemed to shift, symbolic of the tumultuous terrain within Michael's soul. Ellery, grounding herself in the essence of love and understanding, became a beacon amidst his storm, reminiscent of the love Christ symbolized even upon the cross.

"Christ's crucifixion and resurrection," she continued gently, "in the metaphysical lens through Charles Fillmore's interpretations, is an inner journey, from the crucifixion of our lower self – our fears, our shortcomings, our failures – to the resurrection and ascension into our Higher Self, a consciousness of love, understanding, and forgiveness."

Michael, encased in his own shame and guilt, found in Ellery's words a faint flicker of light amidst his darkened tomb.

He whispered, each word a surrender and a plea, "I betrayed myself, Ellery - and you. My fear, my inability to cope with the claustrophobia and pressures, led me to seek solace in the very thing that has now crucified our stability."

Yet, amid the crucifixion of their current reality, Ellery offered a hand, not just in physicality but in spirit, symbolizing an understanding that transcended the moment, as she spoke with gentle authority, "But Dad, resurrection is born from the crucifixions of our lives. Your betrayal is not the end of our story, nor yours. We can find resurrection, a rebirth from this seeming death, by recognizing the Christ within us - our divine capacity to rise above, to love, to forgive, and to begin anew."

Amidst the raw openness of their woundedness, they found a sacred communion, a unity in understanding that their journey, though now shadowed by crucifixion, also held the seeds of resurrection.

Jean-Paul Sartre once said, "Freedom is what you do with

what's been done to you."

Ellery, embodying the wisdom of the ages, offered not condemnation but a path forward, an opportunity for resurrection amidst the crucifixion, understanding that within every ending, within every crucifixion, the seeds of new beginnings – of resurrection – patiently abide, awaiting the nourishment of understanding, love, and the courage to rise anew.

In this sacred space, where crucifixions and resurrections coexist, they found a unity, a silent understanding that they would navigate the path from decay to rebirth, from darkness to light, together.

And so, beneath the enveloping sky, they embarked upon their path of resurrection, their spirits whispering of rebirth amidst the shadows, where love, understanding, and forgiveness illuminated the way forward.

A Prayer

Compassionate Guardian,

As I reflect upon the Last Supper and the betrayal of Jesus, grant me insight into the depths of these events. Teach me to understand the profound lessons of loyalty, sacrifice, and redemption woven through this narrative.

My own moments of betrayal, either by others or by my own actions, help me to find the strength to forgive and grow. Let me learn from Jesus's example of unconditional love and acceptance, even in the face of betrayal.

Guide me to balance my spiritual aspirations with the realities of the material world, ensuring that I do not betray my higher self for fleeting gains. Grant me the wisdom to discern between true spiritual nourishment and the temporary satisfaction of worldly desires.

May the example of Jesus at the Last Supper inspire me to nourish my inner disciples with love, understanding, and spiritual wisdom. Help me to remain true to my spiritual path, even when faced with challenges or temptations.

Amen.

Journaling Prompts

1. **Reflecting on Personal Betrayals:** Think about a time when you felt betrayed or when you betrayed someone else. What were the circumstances, and how did you grow from this experience?

2. **Feeding Your Inner Disciples:** How do you nourish your spiritual self? What practices or beliefs help you maintain a connection to your higher consciousness?

3. **Balancing Spiritual and Material Desires:** Reflect on instances where you've struggled to balance spiritual values and material or ego-driven desires. How did you navigate these moments?

4. **Learning from Jesus's Example:** How does the example of Jesus at the Last Supper inspire you in your daily life, especially in how you treat others and yourself?

5. **Transcending Betrayal:** Consider ways in which you can transcend feelings of betrayal or self-betrayal, transforming these experiences into opportunities for growth and deeper understanding.

Chapter Ten
The Acts of the Apostles

Introduction

The Acts of the Apostles outline the early Christian community's endeavors to spread the teachings of Jesus. From a metaphysical standpoint, it offers insights into collective spiritual evolution and the power of united consciousness.

Traditional Narrative

After receiving the Holy Spirit at Pentecost, the apostles embark on missionary journeys, perform miracles, and establish churches. They face persecution but remain steadfast in spreading the message of Jesus Christ.

Biblical Context

The book of Acts serves as a sequel to the Gospels, capturing the expansion of the early Christian community and the legacy of Jesus's teachings.

Interfaith and Cultural Perspectives

The concept of a divinely inspired community or gathering is common in many religious and spiritual traditions, illustrating the universal quest for collective spiritual growth.

Metaphysical Interpretation

According to Charles Fillmore's Metaphysical Bible Dictionary, the apostles symbolize various aspects of human consciousness that are activated through the indwelling Spirit. The events in Acts exemplify how these aspects can collaborate for greater spiritual actualization.

Quotes and References

Fillmore notes, "The Acts of the Apostles teaches us that when different facets of our consciousness are aligned with Spirit, miraculous transformations can occur."

Real-world Examples

Modern social movements based on principles of love, equality, and justice can be seen as contemporary expressions of the apostolic spirit.

Practical Applications

Strive for unity within your own mind and in your interactions with others, recognizing that collective action inspired by spiritual principles can manifest powerful changes.

Reader Reflections

1. Which "apostolic" qualities do you recognize in yourself?
2. How do you contribute to collective spiritual growth in your community?

Concluding Thoughts

The Acts of the Apostles remind us that we are co-creators in this spiritual journey, capable of great things when aligned with higher consciousness.

Glossary of Metaphysical Interpretations for This Chapter

- Apostles: Facets of human consciousness activated by the Spirit
- Pentecost: The awakening and activation of spiritual faculties
- Holy Spirit: The divine inspiration that empowers human

consciousness

- Missionary Journeys: Efforts to expand one's sphere of spiritual influence

Additional Exercises

1. A guided meditation on integrating various aspects of your consciousness.
2. Journaling prompts to examine how you can actively participate in collective spiritual endeavors.

Chapter Ten

Acts of Love - The Apostles' Journey

Under the luminous embrace of the July sun, Michael, Ellery, and Tillie sauntered through downtown St. Louis, each step a moment of liberation from the constraints and routines that so often enveloped them. Amidst the lively cafés, eclectic shops, and the diversity of human life, they found an unexpected sanctuary—a space where love, kindness, and understanding stitched together a sublime, invisible tapestry.

Strolling past the dignified Arch, its lofty form outlined against the vast, azure sky, Michael initiated a contemplative dialogue, his voice a gentle cascade of thought, "The book of Acts details the apostles' journeys after Jesus ascended, where they communicated his teachings and the embodiment of love he represented to varied lands and peoples."

The physical and metaphysical intersected in this arena of interaction, where the physicality of the Arch served as a metaphor for the invisible bridges constructed through shared stories, acts of kindness, and the universal human experience.

With her eyes reflecting a wellspring of depth and understanding, Ellery responded, "And their true teachings, Dad, resided not just in their words but in their expressions of love and compassion, in embodying the Christ Consciousness, which at its core, is a manifestation of divine love."

Meandering through the various eateries and shops, through the kaleidoscopic blend of people, each embodying their own narratives and dreams, they moved with conscious intent, creating ripples in the collective consciousness through gentle, thoughtful gestures and warm, genuine smiles.

Tillie, with the innate wisdom that belied her years, queried, "Isn't every act of love and kindness we express also a kind of message, Abba? A bit like the apostles, perhaps?"

Michael nodded, a wave of love and reverence for the perceptiveness of his daughter washing over him, "Absolutely, Tillie. Every act of kindness, love, and understanding is our own sermon, where we teach through our actions and presence rather than just our words."

As they navigated through their day, intertwining with the

myriad of lives and stories around them, a quote inspired by Maya Angelou's gently emerged into Michael's consciousness: "People will forget what you said, people will forget what you did, but people will never forget how you made them feel."

This wisdom subtly underscored their experiences, emphasizing that beneath the transience and physicality of their existence, there persisted a spiritual filament, binding them to the Divine and to each other, eternally.

With a mindful pause, Michael embraced the profundity encapsulated within this moment of realization—that their own actions, even those seemingly inconsequential, held the potent capacity to inspire, elevate, and ignite the spark of divine love within others.

Their day, expressed through a symphony of love, connection, and unity, gently reminded them that divine teachings were not merely historical but eternally present, flowing through every act of love, every understanding gesture, and every shared moment of unity, whispering the eternal melody of the divine through the soul of all beings.

A Prayer

Divine Spirit of Oneness,

As I explore the Acts of the Apostles, it inspires me to embrace the spirit of unity and collective spiritual growth. Guide me to understand and embody the apostolic qualities of courage, compassion, and dedication to spreading divine love and wisdom.

Help me to recognize the facets of my own consciousness that align with the apostolic spirit. Empower me to contribute positively to my community, working in harmony with others to create a collective manifestation of Your principles.

Encourage me to seek and value the Holy Spirit's presence in my life, allowing it to guide my actions and inspire my interactions with others. Teach me the importance of community in my spiritual journey, reminding me that together, we can achieve greater heights of spiritual awareness and impact.

In my efforts to spread love, peace, and understanding, let me draw strength and inspiration from the apostolic example, working tirelessly to create a world that reflects Your divine love.

Amen.

Journaling Prompts

1. **Recognizing Apostolic Qualities:** Reflect on the apostolic qualities (e.g., courage, compassion, dedication) you see in yourself. How do you express these qualities in your daily life?

2. **Contribution to Community:** Consider how you currently contribute to the spiritual growth of your community. What more can you do to enhance this contribution?

3. **Learning from the Apostles:** Choose one apostle or an apostolic act from the Acts that resonates with you. What lessons can you learn from this, and how can you apply them in your life?

4. **The Role of the Holy Spirit:** How do you perceive the role of the Holy Spirit in your life? Reflect on moments when you felt divinely inspired or guided.

5. **Unity in Diversity:** The early Christian community was diverse yet united. Reflect on the importance of diversity in your spiritual or religious community and how it contributes to a richer collective experience.

Chapter Eleven
Paul's Conversion

Introduction

Paul's conversion from a zealous persecutor of Christians to one of its most influential apostles is a dramatic transformation story. Metaphysically, it serves as an example of radical change and the shift in consciousness that can occur through divine intervention.

Traditional Narrative

While on the road to Damascus to arrest Christians, Paul is struck by a blinding light and hears the voice of Jesus asking why Paul persecutes Him. This profound experience leads Paul to convert and become a major figure in spreading Christianity.

Biblical Context

This moment is pivotal in the New Testament, illustrating the power of divine grace to effect profound change even in the most unlikely individuals.

Interfaith and Cultural Perspectives

Many religions feature tales of transformation and redemption, signaling the universal potential for spiritual awakening.

Metaphysical Interpretation

In Charles Fillmore's Metaphysical Bible Dictionary, Paul symbolizes the intellectual aspect of humanity that, when enlightened by the Spirit, can become a powerful force for good.

Quotes and References

Fillmore writes, "Paul's conversion shows us that the intellect, when humbled and guided by Spirit, can move from divisiveness to unity."

Real-world Examples

Stories of individuals who have made dramatic life changes after a moment of clarity or near-death experiences can be seen as modern-day parallels to Paul's conversion.

Practical Applications

Take stock of areas in your life where a shift in perspective could lead to greater spiritual or ethical alignment, and be open to those transformative moments.

Reader Reflections

1. Have you ever experienced a profound shift in consciousness similar to Paul's conversion?
2. How can intellectual understanding complement spiritual growth?

Concluding Thoughts

Paul's conversion serves as a reminder that no one is beyond the reach of transformative grace and that the intellect can be a potent tool for spiritual evolution when properly aligned.

Glossary of Metaphysical Interpretations for This Chapter

- Paul: The intellectual aspect of human consciousness
- Damascus Road: The path of transformative experiences
- Blinding Light: Sudden spiritual insight
- Voice of Jesus: The call of higher consciousness

Additional Exercises

1. A guided meditation on embracing transformative experiences.
2. Journaling prompts on moments that led to significant shifts in your beliefs or attitudes.

Chapter Eleven Transformative Journeys - Paul's Conversion

Inside the loft, where urban aesthetics beautifully intertwined with a sense of familial warmth, Michael, Ellery, and Tillie, nestled amidst the tangible and ephemeral memories imbued within the walls, opened a box of Imo's pizza, the inviting aroma intertwining with the gentle ambiance of their home.

Tillie, with sparkling eyes reflecting an insatiable curiosity, turned to Michael and queried, "Abba, you've always mentioned how everyone can change and find a new path. Does that mean anyone can experience a kind of conversion, like Paul in the Bible?"

Michael, gently nodding, replied, "Indeed, Tillie. Paul's conversion on the road to Damascus wasn't merely a historical event, but a symbolic narrative echoing the potential within us all for transformation and revelation, particularly when rooted in spiritual awakening."

Paul's story, transcending the mere physicality of his experience, encapsulated a universal truth: that profound, transformative spiritual experiences could usher forth in unexpected moments, paving new pathways towards understanding, compassion, and divine connection.

As they enjoyed the delightful array of flavors offered by the pizza, Michael further elaborated, "In Charles Fillmore's metaphysical perspective, Paul symbolizes the intellectual or reasoning phase of mind. His conversion exemplifies the profound shift from intellectual rigidity to the luminous path of spiritual understanding and wisdom, underlining that divine truth is accessible to all, even those initially enveloped in resistance or opposition."

The loft, amidst its modern elegance and panoramic

windows offering a captivating view of the bustling life below, cradled their small family in a serene space where profound dialogues and personal transformations subtly unfolded. Here, they could explore the complexities and wonders of life's journey in a sanctuary of love and understanding.

Tillie, ever reflective and possessing a wisdom far beyond her years, gently responded, "So, Abba, our own little conversions, those moments when we choose love, kindness, and understanding over judgment or fear, are our personal roads to Damascus, aren't they?"

A warm, gentle smile adorned Michael's features, "Precisely, Tillie. Every moment, when chosen with consciousness, allows us to experience our own Damascus road, revealing the divine that perpetually resonates within and through us."

The words of philosopher Simone Weil softly echoed through Michael's thoughts: "Attention is the rarest and purest form of generosity." It was in these moments, these intentional acts of being present with his daughters, sharing stories, wisdom, and pondering the profundities of existence, where he found his own continuous, subtle conversions.

The essence of Paul's conversion, witnessed through the lens of metaphysical understanding, beckoned them all to recognize and embrace the divine revelations perpetually unfolding within their daily experiences and choices. It whispered the eternal truth that every act of love, every moment of genuine presence, and every pathway towards understanding represented a sacred, personal journey towards the divine, forever intertwining their souls with the eternal, spiritual dance of existence.

And so, within the heart of the city, inside their loft, amidst slices of pizza and shared glances of love and understanding, Michael, Ellery, and Tillie found their own road to Damascus, illuminating their path with every act of love and every shared moment of spiritual connection.

Chapter Twelve
The Epistles: Love and Faith

Introduction

The Epistles, mainly written by Paul, Peter, John, and others, guide early Christians on how to live a life in line with the teachings of Jesus. From a metaphysical viewpoint, these letters offer timeless wisdom on manifesting love and faith in our lives.

Traditional Narrative

The Epistles are letters that address various issues within the early Christian communities, from moral dilemmas to doctrinal questions. They emphasize the importance of love and faith as cornerstones of Christian living.

Biblical Context

Serving as both instructional guides and theological treatises, the Epistles seeks to clarify complex issues for the early Christian communities.

Interfaith and Cultural Perspectives

Many spiritual traditions offer similar guides and letters, emphasizing love, compassion, and faith as universal spiritual values.

Metaphysical Interpretation

According to Charles Fillmore's Metaphysical Bible Dictionary, love and faith are foundational spiritual attributes. Love represents the drawing power of unity, while faith stands for the substance of things hoped for.

Quotes and References

Fillmore remarks, "Love and faith are like the two wings of the soul, lifting us towards spiritual realization."

Real-world Examples

The practice of loving-kindness in Buddhism or the Sufi teachings on divine love can be seen as parallel spiritual instructions that also focus on love and faith.

Practical Applications

Integrate more acts of love and expressions of faith in your daily life, recognizing that these principles act as catalysts for personal and collective spiritual growth.

Reader Reflections

1. How do you manifest love and faith in your life?
2. What barriers do you encounter in practicing these virtues?

Concluding Thoughts

The Epistles remind us that love and faith are not just emotions or beliefs but active practices that have the power to transform us and the world around us.

Glossary of Metaphysical Interpretations for This Chapter

- Love: The magnetic force of unity and attraction
- Faith: The inner conviction and substance of spiritual realities
- Epistles: Letters or communications of spiritual wisdom
- Community: A reflection of collective consciousness

Additional Exercises

1. A guided meditation focusing on cultivating love and faith.

2. Journaling exercises to explore your personal experiences with these spiritual principles.

Chapter Twelve:

The Epistles - Threads of Love and Faith

Sunlight filters through the charming streets of St. Louis, glimmering across the Mississippi River and offering its gentle embrace to the city. Amidst the dance of light and shadow, Michael and Ellery wandered through the familiar streets, exploring the intricate web of emotions, reflections, and spirituality interwoven with the concrete realities of life.

Today bore a unique significance – a choice to embody symbolism and messages into their very skin through the ancient art of tattooing. Michael, etching "don't care" across his knuckles, and Ellery, choosing a delicate butterfly on her right hand, allowed this moment to become an embodied metaphor, conveying stories of their spiritual and earthly journeys.

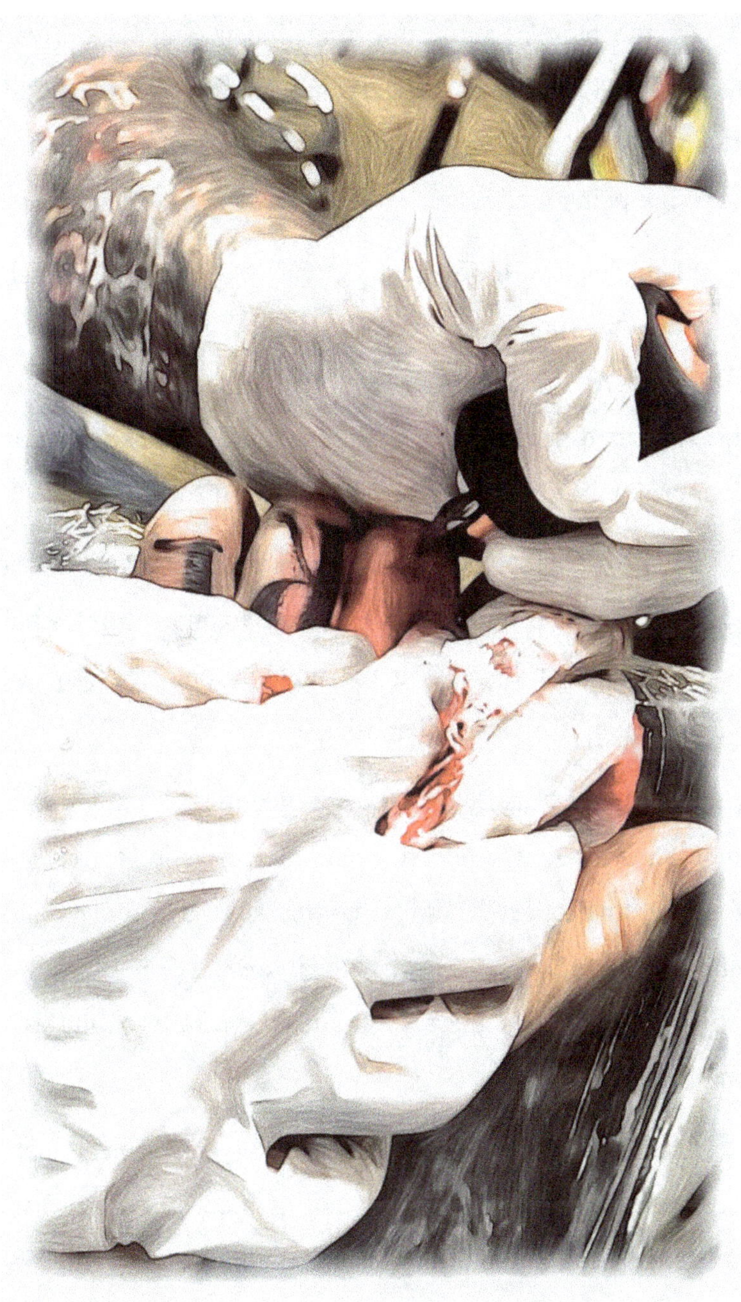

As the hum of the tattoo machine traced the outlines of Michael's knuckles, the rich history and symbolic resonance of the Epistles unraveled in their conversation, meandering through each stroke of ink being meticulously woven into their skin.

"The Epistles, the letters written by apostles such as Paul, Peter, and John, spoke not merely to early Christian communities but echo timeless messages concerning love, faith, and the intrinsic connectivity amongst all beings," Michael softly spoke, his voice a gentle murmur amidst the ambient sounds of the tattoo studio.

Ellery, glancing at her emerging butterfly, pondered, "These messages of love and faith aren't restricted to ancient times but are persistently relevant, mirroring the metamorphic journey we all navigate through life's varied landscapes."

Michael nodded, his eyes reflecting a pool of deep, contemplative thought, "Indeed, Ellery. The Epistles converse with the soul's eternal quest for unity, compassion, and understanding, inviting us all to live in accord with divine love – Agape, which perpetually seeks the highest good and is eternally boundless and unconditioned."

Charles Fillmore, with his metaphysical interpretations, perceived these timeless messages not as mere historical artifacts but as living, breathing entities, perpetually inviting individuals and communities to delve deeper into the divine intricacies of love and faith, recognizing their innate, indomitable power to transform, heal, and unite.

As the ink permeated their skin, forming symbols of rebellious carefreeness and delicate transformation, Michael and Ellery reflected upon how the Epistles, especially Paul's, conveyed profound wisdom and guidance concerning love and faith's role in crafting a soulful, meaningful existence. Paul's words in 1 Corinthians 13:2, "If I have a faith that can move mountains, but do not have love, I am nothing," whispered the eternal truth of love's paramount significance in intertwining the spiritual and earthly realms, ensuring that faith, though profoundly powerful, was forever guided and illuminated by the boundless, unconditioned embrace of Agape.

In the gentle hum of the tattoo machine and the soft, lingering pain that danced with their skins, Michael and Ellery explored the profound realizations that stemmed from these ancient writings – understanding that love and faith, when harmoniously united, offered a transformative power capable of transmuting suffering into wisdom, loss into understanding, and fear into boundless, compassionate love.

Simone de Beauvoir, a French philosopher and writer, once reflected, "One is not born, but rather becomes, a woman." This phrase, though explicitly expressing the existential realization and metamorphosis of women, whispered the universal truth applicable to all beings – that through each choice, every act of love, and every faith-laden step into the unknown, one becomes. One perpetually metamorphoses through life, becoming through each moment of existence.

Their tattoos, now permanently etched into their being, not only symbolized personal meanings and histories but also mirrored the eternal, transformative journey all souls navigate through the earthly experience, perpetually becoming through every act of love and every step of faith.

Emerging from the tattoo studio, their skins adorned with fresh symbols of personal and collective journeys, Michael and Ellery stepped back into the sun-drenched streets of St. Louis, their beings echoing the timeless messages of the Epistles and their skins whispering tales of rebellion, transformation, and the eternal dance of becoming.

In their steps, in their glances, and in their silent, unspoken understanding, love and faith intertwined, crafting a sacred space where the spiritual and earthly eternally embraced, revealing that through every act of love, every choice of faith, and every silently whispered prayer, the divine perpetually echoed through their being, crafting a symphony of existence forever adorned with the boundless, unconditioned embrace of Agape.

And so, amidst the bustling streets of St. Louis, beneath the expansive, eternal sky, and within the silent, sacred spaces of their beings, Michael and Ellery danced with the divine, their souls forever whispering tales of love, faith, and the eternal, metamorphic journey towards the boundless, unconditioned.

The stories from the Epistles and their freshly inked symbols converged, intertwining tales of ancient wisdom with contemporary journeys, forever echoing the universal, timeless dance of souls through the boundless landscapes of love, faith, and eternal becoming.

A Prayer

Divine Source of Light and Wisdom,

As I contemplate the profound conversion of Paul, guide me on my own path of transformation. Illuminate my journey with the light of understanding and open my heart to the profound changes that can occur through Your grace.

Help me to balance my intellectual understanding with spiritual insight, allowing my reasoning mind to be enlightened and guided by Your Spirit. Show me how to use my intellect as a tool for good, spreading love, compassion, and understanding.

Encourage me in moments of doubt or resistance to be open to Your transformative power. May I have the courage to embrace change, especially when it challenges my preconceived notions or beliefs.

Like Paul, let me experience moments of clarity that shift my consciousness and guide me to a higher purpose. Transform my vision so I may see the world through the lens of divine love and wisdom.

Amen.

Journaling Prompts

1. **Reflecting on Personal Transformations:** Think about a moment in your life that was a turning point, similar to Paul's conversion. How did this moment change your beliefs or perspective?

2. **Intellect and Spirituality:** How do you balance your intellectual understanding with your spiritual beliefs? Are there times when one dominates the other?

3. **Moments of Clarity:** Recall a moment of sudden clarity or insight in your life. How did this moment impact your spiritual journey?

4. **Embracing Change:** Consider an area of your life where you might be resisting change. What steps can you take to be more open to transformation in this area?

5. **The Role of Divine Intervention:** Reflect on the role of divine intervention in your life. Do you have experiences where you felt guided or transformed by a higher power?

Chapter Thirteen
The Book of Revelation

Introduction

The Book of Revelation, often seen as enigmatic and perplexing, provides a glimpse into apocalyptic events and the ultimate triumph of good over evil. Metaphysically, it serves as a roadmap for individual and collective spiritual transformation.

Traditional Narrative

Revelation is a prophetic vision given to John, covering the end of the world, the Second Coming of Christ, and the establishment of a new heaven and earth. It's filled with symbolic imagery like the Four Horsemen, the Seven Seals, and the Beast.

Biblical Context

As the final book of the Bible, Revelation seeks to bring closure to the themes and stories that came before it, providing hope and guidance for the future.

Interfaith and Cultural Perspectives

Apocalyptic literature exists in other religious traditions, often serving a similar purpose: to illuminate the path to ultimate spiritual liberation or enlightenment.

Metaphysical Interpretation

In Charles Fillmore's Metaphysical Bible Dictionary, the Book of Revelation is considered an allegory of the soul's journey toward spiritual awakening and unity with the Divine.

Quotes and References

Fillmore states, "Revelation describes the steps, challenges, and triumphs encountered on the soul's spiritual journey."

Real-world Examples

The global challenges we face—climate change, inequality, etc.—can be viewed as external representations of our collective spiritual evolution, much like the apocalyptic scenarios in Revelation.

Practical Applications

Use the teachings of Revelation as a spiritual mirror, reflecting on your own challenges and triumphs in the quest for higher consciousness.

Reader Reflections

1. What symbolic elements in Revelation resonate with your own spiritual journey?
2. How do you interpret the apocalyptic elements in your life?

Concluding Thoughts

Revelation is not just about end times but about new beginnings, reminding us that spiritual growth often comes through trials and tribulations.

Glossary of Metaphysical Interpretations for This Chapter

- Four Horsemen: The four aspects of human consciousness that need to be mastered
- Seven Seals: The seven chakras or energy centers
- Beast: The ego or lower nature
- New Heaven and New Earth: Transformed states of consciousness

Additional Exercises

1. A guided meditation focusing on overcoming personal "apocalypses" to achieve spiritual renewal.
2. Journaling exercises to explore how you deal with trials in your spiritual journey.

Chapter Thirteen:
The Book of Revelations - Departure to Rebirth

The loft basked in the golden hue of the setting sun, a canvas of shadows and memories amidst the boxes and keepsakes. Michael and Ellery moved with intention, each item a testament to their past and a beacon for the future. Tillie was there too, assisting, yet her path was diverging, anchoring her to Illinois as they prepared for their departure.

Ellery, holding an old photo, turned to Michael, "It's like we're living the Book of Revelations, isn't it? Endings intertwined with beginnings." She glanced at Tillie, her eyes soft. "But even as some stories diverge, the essence remains."

Michael nodded, placing a book into a box. "Exactly. Fillmore saw Revelation's visions as symbolic of personal transformation. We're stepping into a new phase, but so is Tillie, in her own way, right here."

Tillie, smiling at the comparison, chimed in, "It's a different kind of apocalypse for me. Not the end of the world, but maybe the end of an era. And I'm okay with that. We're all embarking on new beginnings, even if miles apart."

Their conversation meandered through the packing, each memory a bridge between their shared past and their branching futures. "Kahlil Gibran' once said, "Your living is determined not so much by what life brings to you as by the attitude you bring to life." This resonates now more than ever," Michael reflected. "We're choosing our paths with intention, embracing the journey, each on our routes."

Ellery wrapped a fragile ornament, pondering, "This move, it's more than geographic. It's a spiritual transition for us, and for Tillie too, in her way. Like the rebirth Revelations speaks of, we're all facing our own judgments, deciding what to carry forward and what to leave behind."

The loft gradually emptied, mirroring the transformation within. "Shedding skin isn't just about changing places," Tillie noted, looking around the sparse room. "It's about growth, finding new ground. For you two, it's Miami. For me, it's here, discovering my path."

As the time to part ways drew near, their hearts were heavy yet hopeful. "Miami is our next chapter," Michael said, locking the loft for the last time, "but this isn't goodbye. It's just a different kind of togetherness."

The journey to Miami was a tapestry of thoughts and reflections. Ellery mused, "This road isn't just ours; it's symbolic of every path we choose in life. Uncertain, yes, but filled with the promise of discovery and renewal."

Back in Illinois, Tillie stood firm, her journey intertwined with theirs, yet distinct. "And as you find your new beginning in Miami, I'll be here, crafting my own narrative, keeping the thread that connects us intact."

Their dialogue, rich with the themes of departure and rebirth, underscored the deep bond they shared—a bond not confined by geography but woven through the very fabric of their beings. "Our own Book of Revelations," Michael said, eyes on the horizon, "is about embracing the unknown, trusting in rebirth, and knowing that love and connection transcend distance."

As they neared Miami, the excitement of a new chapter mingled with the sweetness of shared memories. Their story, a testament to enduring bonds and the courage to embrace change, was just beginning anew, framed by the promise of transformation and the unending journey of self-discovery.

A Prayer

Divine Guide Through Times of Change,

As I reflect on the profound messages of the Book of Revelation, guide me through my own spiritual transformation. Illuminate my path as I navigate the trials and tribulations of my life, just as the allegorical visions in Revelation depict the soul's journey through challenge to triumph.

Help me to understand the symbolic meanings behind the apocalyptic imagery, and teach me to apply these lessons to my personal spiritual growth. May I recognize the trials I face as opportunities for transformation and renewal?

Grant me the strength to overcome my personal "beasts" and "horsemen" — the aspects of my consciousness that hinder my spiritual progress. Help me to unlock and balance my inner "seven seals," leading to a greater alignment with Your divine will.

In moments of doubt or despair, remind me that endings are often the precursors to new beginnings and that every challenge I face is a step towards a new heaven and a new earth within my soul.

Amen.

Journaling Prompts

1. **Personal Apocalypses:** Reflect on a personal apocalypse or major life challenge you have faced. How did this experience lead to transformation and growth?

2. **Overcoming Inner Beasts:** Consider the "beasts" in your life — negative habits, thoughts, or behaviors. How can you work to overcome these challenges?

3. **Interpreting Symbolic Imagery:** Choose an image or symbol from Revelation that resonates with you. What does it represent in your life, and how can you learn from it?

4. **Balancing the Seven Seals:** Reflect on the concept of the "seven seals" as aspects of your consciousness. How can you work towards balancing these aspects for greater spiritual harmony?

5. **Triumph of Good over Evil:** How do you see the triumph of good over evil playing out in your own life? What steps can you take to ensure that goodness prevails in your personal journey?

Conclusion

The Eternal Dance of Spiritual Awakening and Metaphysical Insight

The Unending Spiral of Spiritual Unfolding

In our journey through these biblical narratives, enriched by the metaphysical interpretations of Charles Fillmore and the wisdom of various philosophers, we transcend beyond mere words on a page. The experiences of Michael, Ellery, and Tillie mirror an evolution that defies time, space, and physicality, echoing our collective quest for understanding, love, and spiritual enlightenment.

These chapters do not signify an end but mark a continuous spiral, an eternal dance of delving deeper into the realms of metaphysical exploration and spiritual understanding. We are reminded that every conclusion is but a gateway to new beginnings, every perceived ending a rebirth, and each obstacle a stepping stone toward greater wisdom and realization.

As this particular segment of our shared journey closes, the narrative perpetually unfolds into the boundless landscapes of love, faith, and interconnectedness. This journey, both theirs and ours, spirals endlessly into the infinite realms of discovery, where each step, word, and breath is a conscious exploration into the depths of our souls and the omnipresent divine reality.

In Everlasting Love and Eternal Unity

Let this exploration be an invitation to view life as a divine play, to find depth in the mundane, and to discover spiritual truths in everyday challenges. In the words of Blaise Pascal, let us understand the profound reasons of the heart, leading us closer to enlightenment, love, and the eternal embrace of the Divine.

Our journey through these metaphysical landscapes reminds us that life is to be lived forward but can only be understood backward. As we carry these insights into our lives, we continue the unending spiral of spiritual unfolding and metaphysical enlightenment, dancing eternally in the infinite realms of love, spirit, and discovery.

Closing Prayer from Our Family to You, the Reader

Dear Reader,

As we conclude this shared journey, our family extends a prayer from our hearts to yours. May the wisdom and insights you've discovered in these pages resonate deeply within you, illuminating your path with love, understanding, and spiritual growth.

We pray that the metaphysical interpretations of these ancient stories enrich your life, offering new perspectives and deeper connections to the divine. May these teachings foster in you a spirit of compassion, curiosity, and a relentless pursuit of truth.

May you find strength and guidance in the trials and triumphs of your journey, just as we have found in ours. Let the stories and reflections within this book be a source of comfort and inspiration as you navigate the complexities of your own life.

In gratitude and with heartfelt wishes, we send you forth with blessings of peace, joy, and an ever-deepening connection to the spiritual essence that binds us all. May your journey be filled with meaningful discoveries and profound transformations.

With love and blessings,

Mychael, Ellery and Tillie Renn….

Amen.

About the Author

Mychael Renn is a spiritual explorer whose journey traverses the realms of metaphysical inquiry and the profound mysteries of biblical narratives. With a background that spans various disciplines, Renn brings a unique perspective to the spiritual dialogue. His latest work, "Nailed It!!!", is an invitation into the heart of biblical parables, reimagined through a metaphysical lens, offering readers a pathway to personal and spiritual discovery. Renn's narrative is deeply personal, rooted in his transformative experiences and reflective practices, making his insights both accessible and compelling. Through his writing, Renn aspires to bridge the ancient with the contemporary, guiding readers to uncover the deeper spiritual truths that lie within the sacred stories of the past and how they illuminate our paths today. An advocate for spiritual growth and understanding, Renn's work is a testament to the transformative power of viewing life through a spiritual lens, inviting us to explore, question, and find personal meaning in the timeless narratives that shape our existence.

www.ingramcontent.com/pod-product-compliance
Lightning Source LLC
Chambersburg PA
CBHW050314160726
48002CB00001B/24